Praise for Caro

CW00540507

Redefining SELFISH

As a busy, working mum of two young daughters, prioritising 'me time' is something of a joke. Carolyn Hobdey guided me through the process of Redefining SELFISH, and it was eye-opening. I admit to the book setting me off down a path I wasn't expecting. The Elimination section was particularly enlightening. I realised that I had got into some bad habits that were damaging to my long-term health (physical and mental). And because Carolyn has been there, done that, got the t-shirt, it never feels patronising or challenging. Her advice is more like sitting with someone kind and wise, straight-talking but with my best interests at heart, written from the heart, to help women like me regain control and balance. Hugely empowering.
Amazon reviewer

Redefining SELFISH by Carolyn Hobdey is written from the heart.
WorkingMums.co.uk

This book takes an empathetic approach and gives bitesize approaches, it allows you to have kindness and patience with yourself when dealing with life. This is so necessary for everyone to read in life. Highly recommend. Especially loved the reflection to true life to humanise my feelings and relate.
Netgalley reviewer

Thought provoking and motivating. Women are traditionally taught (by society) to stay in their boxes, and this book provides motivation to speak up, redefine yourself. SELFISH, in this book, is used to describe various words which helps with redefining yourself.
Netgalley reviewer

I recommend this book to anyone who is tired of living for others, and not themselves.
Netgalley reviewer

All The Twats I Met Along The Way

By turns funny, incisive and painful, Hobdey's unflinchingly honest account of a series of disastrous relationships will resonate with every woman who has loved unwisely.
Frances Hardy, Daily Mail

This is a bold memoir about a woman falling down, getting back up again, and trying time and time again to become a better person. And she's done it.
Amazon reviewer

The honesty and rawness of Carolyn's words are utterly reassuring. I found myself gripped by her story and better able to assess my own experiences, as I was able to relate to so much of what she had to say.
Amazon reviewer

Blisteringly, searingly honest. How much crap can one person take in a life? Limitless it seems and yet all of Carolyn's story is told with honesty, anguish, sometimes really funny and sometimes the love shines through. But I did notice there never seemed to be a victim's plea. She literally just got straight back up and moved on. And all the time I wanted to turn the page to find the next Twat. Fabulous stuff.
Amazon reviewer

An absorbing read. Honest and thoughtful.
Amazon reviewer

An inspiring, frank and utterly original read that I cannot recommend highly enough.
The Book Doctor

A word of warning before you start to read this book by Harrogate based Carolyn Hobdey - it is highly addictive. I picked up the book to have a quick look through it at 10pm - by 12.30am I was still engrossed in this true tales of awful boyfriends, manipulating men, love triangles and unsupported medical diagnoses.
Lancashire Times

Carolyn Hobdey and her books have been featured in i News, Daily Mail, Scottish Daily Mail, Irish Daily Mail, Daily Mirror, The Sun, Woman's Own, Channel 4's Steph's Packed Lunch, BBC Radio, WeAreHoi, Lancashire Times, Harrogate Examiner, Yorkshire Times, HR Wire, HR Grapevine, Parenting without Tears, Female First, Working Mums, The Successful Founder, North Manchester FM, Family Friendly Working, The Carer, Netdoctor, Wellbeing Radio and more . . .

De-Twat Your Life!

Simple Steps to *Being* Unapologetically your*SELF*

CAROLYN HOBDEY

By The Author School

Published by Ink! Publishing 2022

Typeset in Garamond Classic 11.25/14.5 by
Hewer Text UK Ltd, Edinburgh

ISBN number 978-1-7399703-4-5

By The Author School
ink! By The Author School
Kent, England, United Kingdom
Email: inkpublishingservices@gmail.com
Website: www.inkpublishingservices.co.uk
Twitter: @services_ink

For my Mum, who is my standard-bearer,
and my Dad, who is my hero.
I will carry your strength with me, always.

Contents

Acknowledgements

The difficult second album . . .

I was worried that this same principle applied to second books – in this case, of a trilogy. Writing is both a craft and an art. Like anything that falls into either of those categories, the only way to get better is to keep doing it. I'm still learning. I'm developing my voice and finding my style. None of that would have been possible without the support, challenge and encouragement of a fabulous group of people.

The amazing team at Literally PR—consistently professional, positive and kind. Thank you for the opportunities to write, contribute and speak on various platforms; it has been invaluable experience and I love every gift that you have given me. They are led by the incredible tour-de-force that is Helen Lewis, who also co-runs the publishers for my books, Ink! alongside the great Abiola Bello. Helen, you just 'get' me and believe in my mission. It's always a pleasure to work with you and you fill me full of energy every time we speak.

Thank you to the immensely talented Helen Braid for her illustrations and designs, and to the team at Hewer Text for making it all fit together.

I must recognise the beautiful soul that is Anthea Armar at Amarkai Coaching. Thank you for holding me to account for getting the first draft done and for helping me to understand that creating freedom in others through being a storyteller is my legacy.

My family: you are the foundation upon which I stand. You shelter me during the storms. You ensure the light floods in. I have a lot of words, but never enough to describe my love for you.

My friends: you choose to have me in your lives and for that I am eternally grateful. For their cheerleading in respect of my writing of this particular book, I must call out Susan Slater, Cliff Sewell, Lewis Borlase, James White, Gill Farr, Anthony Downes, Graham Clark, Sarah Ayrton, Olivia Eaglen and Jo Britton (for encouraging me to De-Twat the world!). Thanks to you all for always asking how it's going, even when sometimes my reply has been just to roll my eyes!

As the saying goes, *"people come into our lives for a reason, a season or a lifetime"*. I have experienced all of those whilst writing this book and I am grateful to every one of them for the experiences and richness they have brought to my world. After all, when you're a writer, *everything* is content . . . anyone who encounters me ought to be aware of that!

"To attract better, you have to become better.
You can't do the same things and expect change.
Transform your mindset.
Upgrade your habits.
Think positive.
Be hopeful and consistent with your evolution.
It all starts with you and how you feel about yourself."
- @idillionaire -

Does this sound familiar?

Does your life 'look' good? Do you have all the accepted tenets of success? Do you have every reason to *be* grateful?

And yet, there's a bit of a niggle . . . an itch that you just want to scratch.

Because something just doesn't seem 'right'. How things look and how you feel aren't in sync.

You feel guilty for saying it. In fact, you may not have said it out loud to anyone. Not even to yourself.

But you look at your life and think, "is this it?".

It's OK. You're safe here. You can say that. Without judgement from me.

I recognise that deflating feeling when each day looks like the next. Weeks merge. They turn into years. You carry a general feeling of malaise that all the holidays, shoes, nights out, cocktails and beautifully put together home interiors can't manage to erase. You can't help thinking that things might just feel the way they do today until . . . well, until you die.

That the Grim Reaper might just show up and say, "I'm taking you now for your own good. Life is wasted on those who don't actually *live*".

Ouch. Harsh, but true.

The idea that you've not stepped into who you are. That you've dimmed your light. Not reached your early potential. That you've people-pleased your way through life. Put up with stuff that you shouldn't have. Let go of your dreams (forgotten what they were, even). In short, that you've both endured Twats and been one. That doesn't feel much like a well-lived life, does it? That's not fulfilment. It's an existence. Conforming to societal expectations and ticking every box of what life 'should' look like.

Should.

Ought.

Must.

Pleasant, but unremarkable.

Vanilla.

I don't think you were put here to be vanilla. You weren't meant for a life of 'shoulds'. What happened to the ballsy badass that used to rule the playground? The one who was going to take on the world and not put up with any crap in the process. When did they leave?

Fact is, they didn't. They learnt to conform. Shrank. Reduced their wattage.

But they're still there. Waiting. Looking for that moment to shine again.

Reality is, only *you* can create that moment. No-one is going to gift it to you. No-one is going to hand it to you on a plate. I know, it sucks, right? There ain't no short-cut. No cavalry is riding over the hill to save you.

I am going to take you by the hand, though. Lead you there. Walk by your side.

To where? Where are we going?

To a place where your life has meaning. A place where your life is made up of the things and people you want it to contain. A place where you are *Being* yourSELF. Unapologetically.

It's a magical place. But it's NOT a mythical place. It exists. It's real if you make it so.

We're going to FULFILMENT.

Yet, how do you even work out what fulfilment is? Let alone how to get there!

That's where I come in. Your guide. The Midlife Mistress. A passionate life transformationalist.

Why should you trust me with your journey? It's a good question. A wise one. Never go off with a stranger, right?

I'll tell you why you should trust me.

Because once upon a time, I was you.

Lost. Weary. Wary. Lacking confidence. Staying silent. Trapped. Craving change, but not knowing how.

Surrounded by Twats. And being one—especially to myself.

So, if . . .

- You're asking yourself whether your daily grind is making you happy.
- You're left wondering whether the 'juice is worth the squeeze'.
- You've begun to question what your life is all about.
- The people around you feel less like a circle and more like a cage.
- That niggle has become, well, more niggly . . . (look, I know I'm an 'author', but it doesn't mean I get *every* word right, OK?!)
- You're tired of tolerating Twats.

Then this book is for you.

It's about a life you choose.

It's about *Being* yourSELF.

Best of all, it's being totally fucking* Unapologetic.

* sorry for swearing#

but be prepared for more ;)

"Don't let the concept of change scare you
as much as the prospect of remaining unhappy."
- Unknown -

Why did I write this book?

If the COVID-19 global pandemic taught us anything, it was how precarious our lives are. We always knew that, of course, yet one of the myriad frailties of the human condition is that the very thing we have no idea how much of it we have— TIME—is the very thing we waste with absolute abandon.

We throw it away carelessly like we have an infinite supply, even though it is the one commodity that we know we will all run out of. Whilst we jump on the bandwagons of sustainability, renewable energy and the loss of our Earth's natural resources and get—quite rightly—agitated about these causes, we see the diminishing of our own personal reserves as inconsequential.

Odd, when you think about it.

It frequently takes some kind of momentous wake-up call to remind us that we shouldn't be playing fast and loose with our time. Enter stage left: Coronavirus.

What the daily-reported death toll, the months in lockdown and the almost total removal of 'normal' life did, was remind us that we cannot take life or, indeed, our freedom for granted.

You wouldn't be alone if months of home-schooling, endless virtual meetings from your dining table and a constant household argument about internet bandwidth made you reassess what matters to you.

The one thing I was slightly ahead with when Coronavirus hit, was that *my* wake-up call happened two years prior.

You may or may not have read the first book of my 'Twats Trilogy' called 'All The Twats I Met Along The Way'. For those of you who haven't read it, or have, but may have forgotten (that's OK, by the way; your life is busy!) it is a memoir. It's about the years from my mid-teens until mid 2018, when my life spectacularly imploded. The story charts how the low self-worth that was set in place when I was a child led to some very poor choices in my personal life, despite having a successful academic and corporate career in Human Resources. My life was the classic paradox, but each infiltrated the other to create a bit of a mess. So much so that I lost everything—job, relationship, home, step-family—in the space of 10 days. Suicide beckoned. SPOILER ALERT: I didn't succeed. Huge thanks again to the person that saved me.

There's a lot more to the book because if there wasn't that synopsis means the other 100,000 words I wrote were (ironically) a waste of—you guessed it—time.

I wrote the first 'Twats' book because I thought the story was important. Not because I think I am important. Not to anyone other than me at any rate. We are all, let's be honest, the centre of our own universe despite how much we like to think we believe otherwise. No, I thought it was important because my account is a no-holds-barred look at how we talk to ourselves in our own heads. We never talk to anyone as much as we do ourselves. In doing so we frequently tell ourselves unhelpful stories about us, others and their perceptions of us. Mostly when those others actually don't give us a second thought. The purpose of 'All The Twats I Met Along The Way' was to shine a light into the dark recesses of our minds and to address the often poor decisions we make as a result of the thoughts and feelings that lurk there. Most of which are warped nonsense. Whilst I'd felt very alone with those thoughts during much of my life's journey, what happened after the world as I'd known it caved in, made me realise that I wasn't. I decided to share my raw story to create a space for others to share theirs; whatever 'theirs' may look like.

As the title suggests, I met a number of Twats along the way in my life, but it's fair to say that at times I was a twat too. The book is no more a glorification of my actions than it is to paint me as a victim, which I don't perceive myself to be. It turns out I was a twat to myself more than anyone else. I frequently inflicted self-harm inside my mind and was cruel with how hard I drove myself physically. I didn't think I had any value, so I threw the door open for others to treat me as if I had none too.

In July 2018 the universe clearly decided that my succession of poor choices and the lack of lessons I was learning, was irritating it. Enough was enough, it thought, and issued me with one almighty kick up the arse. It was the start of a considerable reset. Mostly a reset of me and who I was. Although it's fair to say that by that stage I didn't really know who I was, so first I had to establish an identity before I did much else. I didn't know how to be *me*.

When I was left with no job, no relationship, no home and no (step) children, I really became a blank canvas. The world was, as the saying goes, my oyster. Whilst that may sound exciting, in that moment—when I was totally destabilised—that thought was terrifying. I didn't know how to 'be' without those things around me. They were the very essence of my being, or so I thought, and I believed I was nobody without them. Not least my work, which had been a mainstay through some very turbulent times in my private life. That's not to say that the work part was easy—far from it! It was challenging. It was emotionally and physically gruelling, and, on a couple of occasions, my work and personal stuff were one and the same —more of that elsewhere in my trilogy . . .

After my life was razed to the ground, I felt like I had very few choices. If any. Having been saved from the most terminal of those limited options by a very special group of friends, I then had to choose between hiding under the duvet whilst hoping it would all go away or—as my best friend would so eloquently put it—to "pick my knickers up and box on". Ironic how, in the process of my recovery, actual boxing became an integral part of my recovery, but I'll say more about that another time. Suffice it to say, hiding under the duvet was not a viable option. Life is a constant journey with various way markers and it was inevitable that I couldn't languish in the same place for the rest of my days, however much I wanted to. The world keeps turning and things consistently evolve. I had to get on with adulting. I had to work out the way forward. I was totally lost, being tossed about by my emotions, my situation, and the fact that I had nothing stable to cling to. There was no 'losing everything' guide to consult. Believe me, I tried Googling that!

Suddenly.

Abruptly.

Nothing.

Everywhere I turned I peered into fog. I couldn't think straight. I couldn't see straight. I was discombobulated. It was like living in a permanent disaster movie: out on open water, exposed, vulnerable, mist swirling . . . the light would form shapes that I couldn't fathom and I felt perpetually like I was seeing deceptions of a world that I was no longer part of.

What I was experiencing was heartbreak.

In its cruellest, most absolute form. If you've ever endured it, you'll know how it hijacks your entire being and convinces your body that you're losing your mind. But it was more than that. Combined with my romantic heartbreak was grief at the loss of every dream I'd ever had about having a family. The tearing of my step-children from me was as though my heart had been ripped from my chest through my throat. The pain was so immense that I couldn't even cry. The sob that tore at my soul was so intense that no sound came out. A scream that came from so deep within that by the time it reached my lips it couldn't be uttered. It was a primal loss.

You may be thinking, "But they were not your children". They weren't. I'd known that. I was, essentially, nothing to them. I'd always treated any time that I got to be 'something' in their lives as an absolute privilege. Never as a given or a right or to be taken for granted. I knew that they were only ever on loan from their real mothers. The only tie was their father; that was why I had entered their life and the reason I had remained in it. His decision to end our relationship was why I was no longer there.

However, nothing that I tried to reason my way through could assuage the grief. I'd loved them unconditionally. Even though their father had used the threat of their removal as an emotional weapon for large parts of our relationship, I'd loved them like they were my own. I'd been powerless to prevent that. I'd loved them more than I imagined I might have loved my own children because they had been a gift that my inability to conceive had never dared to dream I would ever receive. They allowed me to love in a way I didn't think I would be permitted to in my life. That basic maternal instinct had overridden any logic. Now I was paying the price. It was costly.

Then there was the heartbreak for my work. It had been my life. It was the thing I had thrown myself into when other parts of my life had been in disarray. This latest role had been about the most special of them all. My pride in the team I'd built, in particular. My heartbreak was for leaving those wonderful people behind. Not least because I felt like I was abandoning them to a regime that didn't care for them or value the important work that they did. I was passionately protective of them. I cared about them as individuals. I was so invested in what we were trying to build as a group. To be cast out from the organisation with barely time to say my goodbyes was like being wrenched from the arms of my family. Not least because the reason I had to leave was due to the actions of someone else, but as is so often the case when a business has to ultimately choose between its people and its profits, suddenly its conscience takes a vacation. I felt so betrayed. Everything that I'd been assured the organisation stood for slipped through my fingers like sand.

My greatest heartbreak of all was with myself. I had become something that I didn't think was possible. I'd become the woman who apologised for things she'd not done. A woman who placated her partner to avoid a row. I had become that woman who had done everything to sooth his temper at the expense of any self-respect. I had stayed silent. Had absorbed the emotional punches and perfected the art of not flinching. Mostly. Had sacrificed my worth at the altar of relationship gratitude. I hated myself for becoming a snivelling example of servitude to the need to be with someone. I was filled with self-derision at those choices. Not just with him, but his predecessors also.

In the throes of my heartbreak, my identity fell to the floor like the beads of a broken necklace; each tiny fragment of glass bouncing off the hard surface of my pain and scattering in every direction. Whilst I fell to my knees in response, I was too shattered to attempt to crawl around to find the disparate pieces. I was in darkness. Exhausted. The emptiness inside meant I couldn't bring myself to care.

Where was I even meant to begin in dragging myself out of the place that had resulted in me just wanting to lie down and stop breathing?

That's the purpose of this book.

I stumbled around in the confusion of my up-ended world for months. Longer. Through necessity, I began to get my act together. I can promise you, it did NOT feel like I was. Nothing made any sense. My brain felt like candy floss. My previous mental capacity seemed to have evaporated. It was as though I could only view the world through the lens of my various forms of devastation and it totally dictated every choice I made. When my heartbreak made me sad, when it made me angry, when it meant I was lost and when I tried desperately to find solid ground. It was there.

I made some wise choices.

I made some really bloody stupid choices!

In doing both I learnt a tonne of stuff. About myself. About other people. And about Twats.

I'm going to share those lessons with you. Even though that's hard.

I'm doing it, though, because that is the point of this book.

I get to share what I learnt having lost my way, having had others misdirect me, having encountered numerous dead-ends and having found my way out. Well, having found my way out it in as much as I reached a new, better 'start' point from whence to keep moving onwards (see, I struggle to find a word so I end up with 'niggly', then I go and throw in a posh word like 'whence' – get me! Anyway, back to it). In that initial phase, however, I did, make a huge transformation. When I was able to look back across it from the standpoint of being a much-stabilised version of me, I could make sense of the decisions and processes that had got me there. That's what this book sets out: the Steps I took to deal with change in my life to help you make change in yours. Whether that change is by choice or by circumstance, it doesn't matter. Whatever way you've come about that change, I have developed the 'How To' guide to step into *Being* yourSELF based on my own, lived experience. I've done the work on the process so that you don't have to. Change is hard enough so take the path of least resistance where you can!

That process is called 'SELF'.

This book sets out the SELF Steps.

Its purpose is to help you to assess and update your life in as controlled and thoughtful a way as possible under what may be challenging circumstances, especially if there is an urgency to make some changes. Rather than you flailing around and being dragged along by the momentum of daily life, the SELF Steps are each designed to carry you forward to the next safe haven where you can catch your breath.

I'll be honest in saying that when my life got turned upside down, I didn't do the Steps in the order that I have laid them out in the SELF structure. That may be an obvious thing to say, but it's worth stating specifically. I got stuck in places. I circled back on myself. I got lost. I took the long way round. All of those things, however, are the reasons why I learnt so deeply what I should (and shouldn't) have done. And with whom!

Through detailing this process, I intend to help save your most precious commodity - *time*.

This is the point in proceedings where I get to be less maudlin about what led to me to write this book and start, instead, to unveil the SELF Steps. In doing so I get to tell the stories behind how each element came into being. Some of those stories are of trials and some are of triumphs, but they all provided the perspective needed.

In 'All The Twats' I laid myself bare. It was a raw, honest—like, cringingly honest—account of my life. I continue that approach here. That's because I cannot ask you to delve deep into you and your life unless I demonstrate that I am prepared to do the same. I cannot expect you to immerse yourself in this process, which will undoubtedly make you uncomfortable at times, unless I am prepared to be uncomfortable too. I'll be honest— because that's my 'thing', clearly—and say that it is even harder to do that here than it was in my first book in the Twats Trilogy. Why? Because the things I learnt during my transformation were frequently bloody tough. Yet, there were many things in my life until that point that had been difficult and I still managed to write openly about them. Here, however, it has been different because what I write about is still recent at the time of going to print. It turns out there is a large dollop of proximity when it comes to our level of pain. I promised myself during that transformation, however, that I would live my life from there onwards as unapologetically me. That's not to say that I would never apologise – of course I would if I had done something wrong or upset someone – but I was going to live life *Being* mySELF. That's what I am here to help you do and why I know what you need to do.

But need to do what, exactly?

"Why can't you just be happy with what you have?
You can be wildly happy with what you have,
and still strive to grow and contribute.
So don't ever let anyone discourage you
from your ambition for a better life."
- **Brendon Burchard** -

Why do you need this book?

My huge passion is that we all have the right to live the life that's right for us. A fulfilled life. To choose who we are and to live as that person. *Being* yourSELF.

I spent my life trying to live up to others' expectations. Not really any one, single person's expectations. Just life's expectations. What society tells us 'success' looks like. It wasn't so much that I didn't have any other choice, more that I didn't really perceive there was an alternative.

- House.
- Car.
- Job.
- Family.

I thought if I simply ticked all those boxes then I'd have life sussed. I'd be fulfilled. I'd have made it.

How wrong I was!

Let's be clear. There's nothing wrong with that tick-list. Nothing at all. If it's what puts fire in your belly and enables you to look back on your time in this world with the satisfaction that you've had a well-lived life, then great. Seriously, that's brilliant. Indeed, those things in your life may well be the basic foundations of your wants and needs. That's perfectly acceptable. Like I said, no judgement about what you choose. Good for you if having those things works for you and you feel totally satisfied. What we're concerned with here, though, is HOW you live that life. Have you taken time to look at it? *Really* look at it. How does your life feel? Are you fulfilled? Is it meaningful? Are you living it the way you want? Are you being true to you?

Frequently, we don't stop to ask ourselves these questions. If they do arise, there is a tendency to push them away and not confront the answers. We might feel guilty for even questioning the life we have, especially if the house is lovely, the job pays well, you drive a decent car and have family around you.

Why wouldn't we be grateful to have all that?

All of those items on that tick-list may even have been what you had in mind when you embarked on 'adulthood'. But who's list was it? Who's vision of fulfilment? Did you stop to think about how it would feel when you achieved it? Does the reality match that?

Now, I'm not advocating that you abandon your life and run away with the circus - to coin a phrase. Yet, I did write this book for those who sit and survey their life and just have an itch that they cannot ignore. An itch that tells them that what they have just isn't quite what they want. Something just isn't working. More than anything, it's for those who don't know *why* they feel like that.

Frequently, we're led to believe that we should just have life all figured out. It's why we have the 'Happiness Tick-list' approach: tick all these boxes and you'll be happy. The thing is, though, that when we don't define for ourselves what makes *us* happy then external expectations ultimately just don't cut it. Let me clarify, by 'happy', I actually mean 'fulfilled'. That's because happiness is a temporary state that fluctuates, whereas fulfilment is stable and maintains our passion and interest during happy times or sad. It's this definition that explains why the generic 'happy life' blueprint is a one-size-fits-all that actually fits very few people, if truth be told. It's simply that we frequently don't feel able to articulate that truth. Our truth. It takes courage to stick your head above the proverbial parapet and say you're not fulfilled; that perhaps your life doesn't quite have the right contents to make it meaningful for YOU.

It may be that you've been thrust into having a re-think of your life after some significant event: redundancy, bereavement, relationship breakdown, etc. Instead, perhaps you've simply reached that midlife point that makes most people stop and contemplate their past versus their future. Whatever your situation, it can be tempting to cling to what is familiar rather than embrace the opportunity that these disruptions represent; that's certainly what happened to me, initially, at least. Until fulfilling that tick-list became . . . unfulfilling.

So, let me talk about what happens next in this book.

Its purpose is to take you on a journey from the life you have to the life you want. The right life. A fulfilled life. One where you are being unapologetically you.

Now, that's easier said than done, I know. So the aim of this book, as I said previously, is to take away the need for you to worry about the 'how to' of that process and instead concentrate your efforts on putting in the thought and feelings required to work through its Steps.

This is a step-by-step guide. That's not to say that the process is perfectly linear. You need to be prepared that it's not. Sometimes you'll need to circle back and revisit some of your thinking. It's an iterative process. You may need to zigzag a little to reach your destination; be open to adjust and amend as you go. This is absolutely usual and should be expected, so start with that mindset. As you evolve and delve, the more information will come to light; this will help you to continuously refine what you want and who you are so that you can adapt your route to ensure you achieve it.

What they are, though, are Steps. The SELF Steps. You just need to trust that each one will bring progress.

To help you do that I'll outline why each Step is there. It's entirely borne from my own experience and just like in my book, 'All The Twats I Met Along The Way', my intention is to be searingly honest about that experience. I call it out here so that you have the comfort of knowing that our lives, our thoughts and our actions can be messy for us all. It's called being human. I tell it this way not so that I can prevent you making *any* mistakes, but in the hope that by gifting you the benefit of mine you might just have a smoother transition.

Let's not waste any more time.

How do you get the most out of this book?

The first time you engage with the SELF Steps it is definitely a process that you need to go through in order. This is so that the picture builds and develops as you work through it. As I mentioned, it's not a linear process because our lives don't work like that; we learn and experience new things that give us additional information. This is why you might find yourself going back and building on or adding to your thinking in one Step, once you've done some reflecting as a result of an exercise in another Step. However, working through each of the Steps in their intended sequence initially will help you to build the most complete first blueprint that you can then start to enact. As you do that you might find there are particular Steps, or activities within Steps, that you want to revisit to go to a deeper level.

It is certainly designed as an iterative, ongoing process of determining a direction, defining the actions to take to reach a certain destination and then building upon that success to determine where to go next with it.

Our lives are extremely busy—full of demands and distractions—so it's important that we start from a place of understanding this and are, therefore, realistic about what we're able to commit to. If we overcommit—often in a first flush of enthusiasm—we may fall at the first hurdle, and then we're more likely to throw in the towel and give up. Precious time is then wasted waiting for the urge to do something about what isn't right in our life to get so strong that you can no longer contain it; then you start again. Taking up a new exercise regime is a great example of where we do this. Let's learn from that by recognising that small, incremental, manageable portions of progress (that, ideally, we schedule into our existing routines, but more of that later) is the best route to long-term success. After all, you don't go to the gym once and then ask, "where are my muscles?!".

To apply this approach practically to the rest of this book, I'd recommend that you carve out small chunks of regular time that you commit to protecting and keeping sacred in your schedule, as best you can. The SELF Steps involve thinking and connecting with your emotions, so uninterrupted time is what you will want to aim for. Think about where and at what time of day that is most achievable for you. If you invest those small increments of time, you will reap the rewards.

Finally, a few words about partnering. You may choose to work with others on some of the activities in the book or in sharing your outputs; that may be a friend, a family member, someone from a group you belong to or someone at work. Whoever it is, I want you to select them very carefully and consider what you want to share. I'd like you to remember that *you* are undertaking this journey for yourself. It needs to be done by you and for you. That's not to say that the inputs and perspectives of others aren't helpful but think about that person's agenda. How comfortable will they be with what you have to say or plan to do? What experiences have they had in their life—that you may or may not be aware of—that might shape their view of what you're doing? Particularly remember that those who care about us most sometimes find the idea of *us* doing or becoming something different is uncomfortable or difficult for *them*—not because they have many ill-intent—but because they love us as we are at the moment. They will want to keep us safe from what they perceive as harm. Be mindful that the idea that we might not like who we are or where we're at in our lives, or that making adjustments might be challenging for us at times, may mean that they present opinions based on their need to protect us from that. Just some things to consider along the way.

The Practical Stuff
There is no point of intention without action. That's why at the end of each SELF Step you will find some practical activities for you to do. This will ensure that you implement the Steps and see results.

All of these exercises are designed to be completed on a piece of paper or electronically if you wish to do them that way. To aid you there are downloadable documents for some of the activities (both editable and printable) that provide structure and further guidance. These are available at:

www.carolynhobdey.com/SELF/resources

I hope you find these activities useful.

I wish you every success as you take your first SELF Step.

What are the stages of Being yourSELF?

A major part of my life-reset in 2018 was learning that I mattered. That attending to me was an important part of being my best going forward. Having felt like I had lost my way—both in life and as a person—being who I wanted to be in a life that I chose was suddenly vital. Everything that I thought that success was meant nothing if I was too run down, weary and fed up to embrace it.

I'd spent so long de-prioritising myself and my needs—always in favour of pleasing somebody else, whether at home or at work—that I'd lost sight of who I was and was woeful at taking care of me. It's where the concept of SELF came from.

After I wrote 'All The Twats', I wrote another book called 'Redefining SELFISH. No Guilt. No Regrets.', which was the precursor to the more in-depth SELF model. Redefining SELFISH is based on the premise that if we don't first attend to ourselves, everything else around us can end up being a bit rubbish—frequently we don't realise why. We don't always appreciate that this is due to social conditioning; that conditioning tells us that subjugating our needs for the sake of others is virtuous. That somehow bending ourselves out of shape to be everything to everyone and present a vision of a perfect life is the ultimate aspiration. I do have to say, this expectation is placed more squarely, but not exclusively, on the shoulders of women, which is why 'Redefining SELFISH' was aimed more at that audience. The book itself was conceived from the fact that I disagree with the idea that putting everyone else above ourselves is a good thing. In fact,

I think it's a very bad thing. If we always put ourselves at the bottom of our 'to-do' list, become our lowest priority, and don't attend to our own self-care/self-kindness—whatever you want to call it—then we reinforce to ourselves that we don't matter. That, in turn, will be how we get treated by others.

What Redefining SELFISH does, is provide a first-rung-of-the-ladder introduction—a bit of a flirtation, if you will—to the shift in mindset that is needed when we want a different life. It gives practical advice, as well as activities, to get started with dipping your toe in the water to see the benefits of placing you as a priority. It introduces the idea that if you want to love and care for others, to look after them, support them and be there for them, then you have to put yourself in a position to do that to the best of your ability. That cannot be achieved if you're feeling resentful and run-ragged. That's just logical.

There is good reason on a plane or boat that the emergency procedure instructs you to "put on your own life vest before helping others" (which even applies to helping your children too) because we are no use to anyone if we're struggling to breathe or keep our head above water.

That has definitely been me at various stages in my life. I struggled. I stayed silent. I was selfless. It didn't do me any good.

So, I began by redefining what we understand 'selfish' to mean. Seeing it, instead, as a way of becoming the best version of you for others, by starting with you. As I worked on that, both personally and as a concept, it brought clarity to what the Steps had been that I had taken when I—and my life—had needed to be different. What I saw when I looked back was that there had been four distinct areas of my transformation to actually *BEING* selfish: the shift from altering my thinking to taking action to implement a different life. It all started with me. With mySELF.

I'd needed to understand where I was starting from and where I was wanting to get to (Seeking). Next, I had to articulate who I was and what mattered to me (Expression). Then, I developed a sense of how I wanted to live my life and with whom (Love). Finally, it was about putting that purpose into action (Fulfilment) to bring about that change and live as me.

1. SELF-Seeking: *where* am I?
2. SELF-Expression: *who* am I?
3. SELF-Love: *how* am I?
4. SELF-Fulfilment: *when* am I?

Hence 'SELF'.

It's why this book is a continuation of the 'Twats' theme: the ones you'll need to deal with, the one you may sometimes be to yourself and others, and the ones who are anything but who you need to spot and nurture in your life. We'll pay special attention to that last group later.

I created the SELF Steps only after I was able to view what I had gone through from the perspective of a place of safety. A place where I was able to look back and see the things I had done with a clarity that eluded me whilst I was being tossed about in my own personal turmoil. It's a blend of things I did thoughtfully and thoughtlessly at the time. It includes the lessons I learnt prior to the life-implosion that I hadn't much been able to make sense of until I needed them. It involves what I picked up as I went along; small places of sanctuary that appeared as and when they were required that I clung to for some temporary respite. There is plenty in my story of things I did that dragged me down when it was unnecessary for that to happen, so I share those too as words from the wise!

My point being that this isn't out of a textbook. It's not just theory. It's practical. It's learnt from real life.

You know that the SELF Steps come in four stages. Next is that each stage has three Steps within it. This assists with breaking down the process. Making each Step the sole focus at that particular time. It's designed to be manageable. Trying to avoid becoming overwhelmed. I'm not saying that you'll avoid overwhelm altogether, but we can minimise it by seeing the Steps as individual squares; visiting one at a time. Land on it. Stand on it. Get your bearings. Then set off again. Within each Step is a few activities that breaks it down further still. You can go as fast or slow as you choose.

Let me start by describing the four stages.

1: (SELF) Seeking: Where am I?

> *"If you don't know where you are going,*
> *any road will get you there."*
> **- Lewis Carroll -**

As much as I agree with Lewis Carroll, I actually think the first part of any journey is about knowing where you are. That's why this first stage helps you understand exactly that.

What is the problem, exactly? Why is it that you feel like something in your life just isn't 'right'? That's the natural start point. An unflinching honesty about your current situation.

I'm going to level with you.

It takes guts to do this. You have to be prepared to take a proper look at the life you have now: what's working for you and what's not. Then compare that to an imagined life. An ideal life. Not a perfect life—that's something different and, bluntly, unattainable—but a life that is made up of the elements and people that you would choose to have there. Now, this might *sound* easy, but it's not. It involves you explaining in detail what that looks like: what do you want to be known for and what path will your life take? It requires you to get beyond the 'I want to win the lottery/be rich/live in a mansion' knee-jerk reaction that most of us have when we're asked about the life we'd want. That life is one that we *think* we want . . . it's often not the life we *actually* want, but we'll talk more about that when we get into the individual Steps.

Suffice to say that at the Seeking stage there's a chance for a bit of soul-searching and a big dollop of taking a look in the mirror about the trajectory of your life. It might not be for the faint-hearted, but it's so worthwhile. Believe me.

I talk frequently about how we play fast and loose with the time we have on this planet. I make no apology for raising it again here. Plainly, we cannot afford to mess about. Time is precious. Let's not waste it. In short: don't be a Twat! Seeking is here to help you start to quantify: what does a 'life well-lived' mean to you? What does it look like when you don't have that? The contrast between the two is challenging to look at, but beneficial.

It's like rocket-fuel for the soul.

2: (SELF) Expression: Who am I?

> *"Be yourself; everyone else is already taken."*
> **- Oscar Wilde -**

Having looked at what you want out of life, the second stage is about articulating *who* you are.

Taking a look at what drives and motivates you, we'll delve into your values, behaviours and attitudes so that you have a rounded picture of you and, vitally, your worth. What skills and experiences do you have to draw on? What capabilities have you already acquired? When you allow yourself to just be you, what do you discover? You'll reconnect with your identity by shedding the labels that life places upon you—and you place upon yourself—by getting back to who you really are. This connection is key; it helps build trust in yourself as well as developing strategies against the objections or agendas of others.

Here we also begin to look at who those 'others' are. We'll review the key areas of your life as it is now and see the people that surround you, so you can build a picture of your network. That picture will evolve and you'll make some decisions about it in the subsequent SELF stages.

The final part of Expression requires you to take everything you have learnt and acquired in the Steps so far and make a commitment to who you're going to be going forward.

Immediately. By setting out in writing what you stand for, what you'll accept and not accept in your life (there's that Twat thing again!), you'll make a vital statement about the life you intend to have. This is built on the basis that once you have thought those thoughts, you cannot un-know them. You'll be building the security to own who you are and to defend it in the face of opposition. To support this, we'll examine your boundaries and look at ways in which you might establish new ones, if required.

3: (SELF) Love: How am I?

> *"The true measure of a well-lived life is how well we love . . . and how well we are loved in return."*
> - Cathy Maxwell -

In the previous stage I mentioned that a vital part of the methodology behind the SELF Steps is to understand the people around you. Yep, we're talking Twats! By taking a good look at the network of people you determined in earlier Steps, you can examine who you have in your life, where they show up and what role they play. Doing this helps you to understand where the energy-generators are versus the energy-drainers. Having a life you love, where you're certain and comfortable with *Being* yourSELF, is built upon having the right kind of people around you. *Your* people.

Your Vibe Attracts Your Tribe.

This stage is focused on data-gathering so that decisions can be made about these people and your responses to them. Who is pulling in the same direction as you? Who is

Carolyn Hobdey

sabotaging your efforts? As with so much of the SELF Steps, its purpose is to ensure that the choices we make are conscious. Even if the decision is to make no decision. Even if the choice is to do nothing. Conscious choices give us control, options and reflection points; this is essential when we feel in practical or emotional disarray and like we're being thrown around against our will.

One of the critical activities you'll undertake is to plan for the conversations needed with your current network. These might be difficult conversations, requests for help or informative discussions about where you're trying to get to in life so that others understand your journey. Then they can choose—because everyone else has choices too—to support you or not. Whatever the requirement, this stage ensures you feel prepared for those discussions to be clear and constructive, even when it initially appears that they might be uncomfortable. Developing the confidence to step forward into who you are and to create safe spaces for key conversations is part of you truly living the way you want to live.

4: (SELF) Fulfilment: When am I?

"Sometimes our lives have to be completely shaken up, changed and rearranged to relocate us to the place we are meant to be."
- Unknown -

The hardest part of any transformation is finding the momentum to get started. That's where the three Steps of the final stage, Fulfilment, come in.

It starts by examining all the options you have in front of you in a let-your-imagination-run-wild, remove-all-the-barriers, free-flow of choices, which is then pulled together with a structured analysis of what is possible in order to start building a plan.

This Stage is focused on getting structure and success factors in place so that you can stay true to the plans you've built. Importantly, it entails building coping strategies for when you fall (metaphorically) off the wagon. We all do it. If you plan for sometimes failing and create a positive relationship with the concept of failure, then you can get back on course more quickly and without too much fuss or loss of confidence.

Prioritising what you want or need to tackle first in your life, defining actions with measures and timescales might not sound very exciting, but much of these building blocks are formed in the previous stages; here it is about refinement.

The purpose is to ensure that you understand what 'success' with your plan looks like versus your current perception of success. Also, if you understand what it looks like when you go off track, you can arrest that situation swiftly when it happens.

Frequently, change does not get sustained because these actions and behaviours do not get attended to: we do the work of identifying what needs to happen but fail to nail down the how and when. We have a tendency to rely on the elusive draw of 'willpower'. I'm here to tell you that willpower is not required (yes, shock horror) there will be no willpower necessary for your success. In fact, willpower is nonsense. Yes, really. I'll come back to the things you need to do to eradicate the need for willpower in more detail in this final stage but suffice it to say that by using the SELF Steps, you'll put the right habits and processes in place to ensure your future is the one you want—one you can look back on and celebrate. One that is right for you.

What happens next?
With the 'How To' process laid out for you, your role is to focus on the SELF Steps themselves. Yes, that might be considered self-indulgent. Yes, it's prioritising you. Yes, it's about some introspection. All of that might make you feel a bit uncomfortable—we're kind of programmed to think that dismissing ourselves is a virtue, aren't we? That stiff-upper-lip, being a drudge in our own lives attitude is somehow admirable. What rubbish! What a disrespectful approach to our opportunity at 'life'.

I'm guessing if you've got this far you are now at a crossroads.

Are you ready to quit?

Of course, that is also a choice you have. You can choose to give up at this point because it all sounds too much like hard work and hope that the itch goes away by itself.

Are you ready to continue?

You can also choose to push on because that fire in your belly refuses to be extinguished; you know there is something better out there for you than what you have right now.

Your choice. But ask yourself this: if I told you that ten years from now you'd still be in the same situation that you are today, what would you do? If you're OK with the answer, then there's no need to do anything more. If that question makes you feel even slightly uncomfortable, then keep reading.

> *"Waste your money and you're only out of money but waste your time and you've lost a part of your life."*
> **- Michael LeBoeuf -**

It's time to get going.

Time to not waste any more time.

Time to have a life well-lived.

Time for fulfilment.

What holds us back from making change and what can we do about it?

The thing that will hold you back from making change isn't your ability to enact the Steps required to make it happen. It isn't money or opportunity. It's not that you cannot visualise or articulate what you want. The thing that will prevent you from making change happen is simple: fear.

Dress it up and call it whatever you want, but that's at the root of it.

That's why, before you get going with the Steps, I'm going to take a moment to talk about our fear of change because we all have it to some degree or another. You should at least take some comfort in that. You are not alone in being afraid.

There are many reasons why we can become afraid of contemplating a different future. In turn, these are the things that prevent us from making change. We go back to going through the motions, squash down those niggly feelings for a while (yep, I've used that word again!) telling ourselves it'll be OK. We'll get over it if we just keep pushing forwards. When we all know that, in reality, it's just a matter of time before those feelings of discontent, of something not sitting right with us, are going to resurface.

Therefore, it's important that we understand what it is that we fear, so that we know what might be holding us back.

When we make change, we often have to lose something in order to transition to something else. We can't always keep hold of everything we have and add more new stuff. Life doesn't work that way.

What we 'lose' might be a person that we need to move away from: either minimise or eliminate from our life altogether. It might be a situation at work or at home that we need to alter or put a stop to. We might need to shed labels and identities that we've been holding onto. We might need to leave behind certain beliefs and stories that we tell ourselves: whether those are about us, others or ideas we have about how life 'should' be.

Loss makes us fearful. It is the end of familiarity. Familiarity makes us feel safe. Change is frequently the end of belonging to something or someone. This taps into an innate fear. We have a very primal need to belong to something because, as humans evolved, we learnt that those that were part of communities were those that stood the best chance of survival, usually the *only* chance of survival. Therefore, we have an in-built fear of being cast out from our groups; it triggers our basic survival instincts that have been embedded in our brains since homo sapiens first roamed the Earth.

Facing those fears and accepting the need to lose some things in order to gain others, takes courage. It requires us to address those fears head-on. Making change means that we must hold tightly to the belief that on the other side of it is something better than what we have today. That what you lose will be replaced by a much greater win.

You're here, reading this, about to embark on the SELF Steps because you're ready to stare down those fears. If it helps, rather than viewing this as a change, see it as an 'update', like computer software: see it as going from version 1.0 to version 2.0 of your life. Yes, there might be a few glitches initially, but the new operating system will be far superior once you've become familiar with it.

However you choose to reframe the fear, you already know that the thought of *not* making change makes you more afraid.

Together, let's make it happen.

*"It's OK to be scared.
Being scared means you're about to do
something really, really brave."*
- Mandy Hale -

THE SELF STEPS – STAGE 1

SELF Seeking

Seeking – Who am I?

As we've established, when setting out on any transformational journey you'll struggle to understand where you're going if you don't know where you're starting from. That's where Seeking begins. It's taking stock of the place you're in, then understanding the place you want to get to. Approach this broadly at this point: it's about a sense of direction rather than worrying about the minutiae. Next, you'll anticipate the hazards you may encounter so that you'll be better prepared for them. You'll clarify where they might occur so that your efforts can become a bit more focused. Rather than, "*Everything* is wrong with my life!" you'll be a bit more discerning about what requires your attention.

Clearly, it's always better to be conducting this examination of your life when things are calm and you have adequate space to think straight. We all know, however, that we rarely take the time to do that, either because we are so consumed with getting on with the busy-ness of life or because it falls into the 'difficult to do' bucket. So, we just kinda ignore it until we're forced to take action—even if that is just mental action in the form of thinking through what the hell is happening and what you're going to do!

If you are in the position of taking the time out to do this in a considered way before a wave of 'life' crashes over you, then huge kudos to you. I never did that. I learnt the hard way to do it at this point.

If you're doing this because you can feel a storm brewing, then I hear you! Let's crack on quickly.

If an emergency situation has already hit, then I understand that your brain might feel like mush right now because you're in crisis mode. I'm here to tell you it's going to be OK. You're no longer alone. You'll be pleased to know that I have broken the Steps down to ensure they're quick to grasp and enact if need be. If this is the circumstance you're in, you might want to skip the parts where I explain the story behind each Step and why it is important and come back to that later. Although if you do that, I need you to trust me when I tell you that you need to complete each of these Steps and do so in sequence. Do that, and then return to find out the reasons why, when you've regained some stability.

Wherever you're starting from, let's jump straight in.

SELF Step 1

 AWARENESS

Awareness

What is the story behind this Step?

I've already outlined how midway through 2018 my life caved in and I lost every bit of 'security' that I thought I could rely on. It was the catalyst for enormous change in my life—whether I liked it or not! That change was two-fold. First, I had to find a new home/job and put back in place some structure. Second, but more essentially, I had to completely change myself—by actually working out who I was—in order to avoid going forward with the same mindset/behaviours/habits that had got me to that place. This second part, I discovered, was much harder than the first.

The first I had to get on with due to necessity. My life had been razed to the ground and I needed to pull it back into some semblance of order. The work I needed to do on myself was considerable, but it needed to be carried out at the same time. This was because I was heartbroken and emotionally devastated. Without paying attention to that healing, I

3

wouldn't have been able to move forward with the practical things. For me, they were interdependent.

What I learnt during that transformation of myself significantly influenced a number of the upcoming activities in the SELF Steps, so that particular change will be a recurrent theme in your subsequent reading.

The moment that informed this first Step, Awareness, came many months after the initial implosion and the basic survival activities that were required to get me through the earliest stages of my heartbreak.

That moment happened early in 2019. I was two months into a new job. It was the next big corporate role that was a stage on from the one that I had been ousted from six months previously. I was in the process of buying a stunning five-bedroom house. I had a new car. I was dipping my toe in the dating pool again. I had put in place some new habits and hobbies in my life and was, to any onlooker, sorted.

What I *felt*, though, was uneasy.

I thought it was money. I had long been a money-worrier and, whilst I was excited about my new house, I was taking it on by myself. Perhaps it was the weight of that responsibility. I went back through all my finances with regards to the purchase. They all stacked up. It wasn't that.

The new job was going to be challenging, but nothing I'd not faced into before, so as I considered what lay ahead in that regard I was reassured that I was comfortable that I had the skills to handle that.

Yet, the disquiet didn't quieten.

I couldn't work out why.

It was during a text exchange with my best friend that it finally clicked. Now those of you who have read 'All The Twats' will undoubtedly remember Jen; a considerable personality and the one person who has the ability to ask me the questions I don't want to be asked, but most need to be. Everyone needs a friend like Jen. Since meeting her, I actively try to be that friend to others.

Jen and I were messaging about how we felt about our work—January is a time when many people contemplate the year ahead and think about their jobs after the Christmas break—so nothing unusual there. Yet, I sent a text to Jen that shocked me. It read, '*I don't want to do this fucking shit anymore*'.

I stunned myself. There it was. My epiphany.

The Human Resources career that I had shed blood, sweat and tears over for more than 20 years . . . I'd had enough.

Looking back, I can see now that I was weary. Actually, really fucking exhausted if the truth be told. With all that had happened to me in the previous six months—and loooooong beforehand—I understand now that I was burnt out.

With respect to my professional life in particular, how I felt I now like to describe it this way: I was tired of trying to persuade grown-ups to behave properly. For all its 'tea and toilets' reputation, HR work is hard. You see the worst of humanity—as well as the best, to be fair—and so much of what you do to support people and, frequently, their lives beyond the workplace, is confidential. You rarely get the recognition you deserve and you just absorb the emotional strain of the work itself. Don't get me wrong, I actually *love* HR work. I enjoy working with people. I take pride in improving people's lives, both at work and, as I said, often their home lives too. Shaping companies and teams into something better. I'd just worked so hard for so long: both on the jobs themselves and on the studies to support them. I needed what parents would call a 'time-out'. I needed to stop giving to everyone else and start giving to me.

Since my life had collapsed, what I'd done—very successfully—was to put back in place all the accepted tenets of what a great life looked like. But it wasn't a life I wanted anymore. Not at that moment at least. Not in the same way I had been, and was once again, experiencing it. I was living up to a version of 'happiness' that wasn't making me happy. I actually felt empty. Exhausted by running on the hamster wheel of expectations. I can imagine what you're thinking . . . I had so much to be grateful for. I know that. I was grateful for it in so many ways. I'd had a lifestyle that many would swap a limb for. I feel awful saying it wasn't enough, but it wasn't. I felt like I had so much more to do, to give, to contribute, to achieve in life. I wanted to live *beyond* this version of a great life. In the moments when I was brave enough to lift my line of sight further into my future, all I could see was this same life stretching out before me until retirement. That thought deflated me. In itself it made me feel tired. The fire in my belly, my inner light—whatever you want to call it—dimmed whenever I was brave enough to confront that. I just knew there was more out there for me, even though at the time I didn't know what 'out there' meant.

I know now that the text I sent to Jen was because I was failing to live my 'purpose'. That term gets banded about a lot these days (too much in my opinion) and I have to admit

I find it a bit . . . wanky . . . What I do know and mean is that I was unfulfilled. I find fulfilment a much better word. I felt the way I did because there was, bluntly, something missing in the reason I was getting up every day. I get that sounds like a very 'first-world' problem. Oh, boo hoo, poor me . . . How terrible for me that I was 'unhappy'. OK. I accept that. But let's just pause for a moment. It's why I will always draw the distinction between happiness and fulfilment. The first is a state that fluctuates: it comes and goes as an emotion for all of us. Whereas the second is an underlying constant. Fulfilment is the thing that keeps driving you forward; that you could talk about with anyone at any moment with passion.

Then I take it to the next level. As far as I can tell, whatever theological position you subscribe to, or not, we're all pretty much agreed that this is the only life we get in our current incarnation. As such, I think we all owe it to that opportunity to make our best attempt to live it well. We don't owe it to anyone to dial that down just because they are living their life in their way or, more to the point, in a way that isn't right for them either. As the saying goes: two wrongs don't make a right. That is, don't let someone else make you feel bad for having a well-lived life just because they are not prepared to do what it takes or have the opportunities to do that for themselves.

A well-lived life. *That* is a life of purpose. A life of meaning. A life of fulfilment.

Whatever term works best for you doesn't really matter. I happen to prefer fulfilment because I think we can agree on it describing a *need*. For me, it was this burning desire to understand why I was here—what that need was—that ignited the requirement to do something after that epiphany. I had to know what a 'well-lived life' meant for me. Once I'd thought that thought, I couldn't un-think it. There was no going back.

I think that's why you're here with me too.

Why is this Step important?
The slogan 'living my best life' seems to appear everywhere! Whether it's something we say, printed on merchandise, or added as a hashtag on an online post. I'm sure I've probably used it in the past!

These days I actually find it unhelpful: it's a kind of in-your-face declaration of a perfect life that social media posts would have us believe everyone, except us, is living. The truth is they're not. No one lives their best life all the time.

I believe it's much healthier for us to strive to live the 'right life'—one that we've defined for ourselves that isn't shaped by the standardised expectations of others. One that is a thought-through blend of the things that bring us meaning, and people who positively contribute to that. Not one that is trying to satisfy a tick-list of what is universally viewed as 'success' and based on someone else's definition of an elusive happiness. It's easy to feel confused, uncertain, or even guilty about what that is, however, which is why we start the SELF Steps with 'Awareness'. The activities are designed to provide some definition of what the right life means for you. Exclusively you.

You can only start to live the life you want if you take a moment to articulate what that is. Otherwise it's like setting off on a journey with no idea of your destination—that's hard for you to buy into—let alone get anyone else on board with your travel plan. No-one's going to climb aboard if you tell them you don't have a clue where you're headed, don't possess a map and don't own any navigational equipment!

How do you determine the life you desire?

The initial response when you ask someone how they want their life to look is frequently a flippant one: lots of money, "win the lottery," buy a mansion, sports cars, a helicopter, be on a permanent holiday and a daily shopping spree.

OK, let's take that idea and run with it for a moment.

What if you did win the lottery and became rich beyond your wildest dreams? How would that *actually* be? Would your life feel meaningful? Would the people you have around you now, still be around you then? That last one is a key question. Think about it. Unless you were able and willing, and if they also agreed for you to fund their lifestyle to match yours (and don't assume they would) despite how good it sounds most people don't enjoy being beholden to another to that extent. Chances are that many of your friends, colleagues, and even family, might drift away from your life because of the unequal footing. There's nothing like a grab for money to split people apart. However much you'd like to think it wouldn't. That's the reality of it: you'd have to be prepared that it would bring with it as much loss as gains.

You'd be amazed how many multi-million-pound lottery winners end up lonely and depressed because endless days of shopping and sitting by a pool turn out not to be very satisfying, however appealing it might initially seem.

When we start to look deeper, my experience is that what people are seeking when you ask them to describe their ideal life, isn't about money . . . not lots of it anyway. Of course, people want to feel comfortable financially, not stressed about paying the bills or where the next meal might come from, but once that base is covered, huge wealth is not what determines happiness and definitely not fulfilment. Instead, it is about the connection we have to others, the quality of those relationships and our sense of meaning. Scientific studies have proven that these things actually *increase* our life expectancy. Yes, there is a direct correlation between a fulfilled life with positive relationships and the duration of that life. Paying attention to having a life well-lived means we gain *quantity* as well as quality of time.

A longer life *and* a fulfilled life—who wouldn't say, "yes" to having all that?!

Therefore, you're going to need to dig a little deeper. Really visualise what you want. To begin this, Awareness is about articulating your ideal life.

The Eight Key Life Areas
Let me introduce you to the Eight Key Life Areas. This is the framework I use to provide structure to the examination of our lives. Of course, life doesn't fit neatly into eight buckets, but we naturally compartmentalise the world all the time in order to make sense of it and to stop our brains exploding from the myriad of data we take in through our various senses every second! It's designed to ensure that throughout the activities included in the SELF Steps, you assess each area of your life in a methodical way and don't overlook anything, either inadvertently or deliberately . . .

The table below details each of the eight areas and what aspects of your life should be considered in that element.

Finance: steps you take to ensure your financial security.

 Health and Fitness: activities you do to attend to your physical health.

 Spiritual/Emotional Wellbeing: things you do to look after your mental health.

 Personal Relationships: basically, a euphemism for sex and love – your most intimate relationship (or relationships, we're not judging here).

 Career/Business: any 'work' activity whether or not it is for financial profit.

 Family and Home life: immediate and extended home environments.

 Education/Personal Development: how you grow your knowledge or learn new skills.

 Social and Recreation: friends, hobbies and non-work activities or interests.

These eight elements will crop up several times going forward, so you might want to earmark this page so that you can refer back to it. You can also find a copy to download at www.carolynhobdey.com/SELF/resources

PRACTICAL ACTIVITIES

ACTIVITY 1.1

How do I want my life to be?

The best way to connect with what we want is to visualise it. By creating a strong image and evoking our senses as we do so, we can bring what we want to life in a way that is meaningful to us.

To complete any of the exercises, I would recommend being by yourself in an environment where you have uninterrupted time to think. I know that life is really busy and that, for most of us, there are multiple demands on our time. So, even if you can just get some quiet time for an initial period of 20 to 30 minutes to get out your instinctive thoughts, then do that; you can add to them later as you reflect in the following days.

As a reminder, if you *are* going to partner with anyone to do this exercise, I suggest that it is someone you trust; who you can share your thoughts and emotions with. Choose someone who isn't going to try to shape or influence your outputs. I don't mean that they might do so maliciously, but often those that care about us the most find it hard to listen to our deepest feelings, especially if we are sharing that we are discontented with what we currently have or that we want to make change in our lives. Their instinct will be to protect you from sadness or difficulty and as such they may steer you down the safest path to avoid that, rather than the one that is right, but involves a few challenges along the way.

The first exercise you're going to do is to visualise and then write down your *ideal* life, as if you were living it in the current day. This is done by forming responses to three questions. When you visualise your ideal life, as if you were living it today:

- What do you *see*?
- What do you *hear*?
- What do you *feel*?

Now this might, on the face of it, seem like quite a simple thing to do. What we're looking for here, though, is for you to examine deeply what you want. To state out loud to yourself, maybe for the first time, what *you* want. This is about releasing yourself from the expectations imposed upon you by you or others. It's your 'perfect day', so to speak, the one that consists of all the elements that would bring you fulfilment. It's the way your world would look if you were truly having a well-lived life. Ask: what would it look like if I woke up consistently with excitement about the day ahead or fire in my belly? Only you can know what this is. Only you will know if you are being honest. It may take courage to let this out.

To stimulate some thoughts and ideas for this exercise, refer to the Eight Key Life Areas again. This will prompt you to explore all facets of your potential world so that you don't overlook exploring what you want in any one of them. Remember, this is how you want it to look, so it may involve looking at an area where you don't have anything going on right now.

For a framework document to complete the 'See, Hear and Feel' questions, please visit my website. This document also contains *additional* prompting questions to assist you with getting to the nitty-gritty of what you want. What you will also find in that document is an area for you to explore what you *don't* want. This is included because sometimes it is hard to initially imagine the change you want, so starting with what you wouldn't want your ideal life to contain might be easier to create some momentum in your thinking. This visualisation requires you to be as ruthless about what you'd throw out of your life, as you are specific about what you'd add in.

There is no set way to complete this exercise: do what works for you. For example, you might take each of the three main questions in turn and write down all your thoughts for each one individually before moving onto the next. Alternatively, you might look at the Eight Key Life Areas and write down what you want to see, hear and feel in each one before moving onto the next. What method you use is not important. What matters is getting your thoughts and feelings out so that you can do the second part of the exercise.

The second part is where you take the output of your brainstorm and summarise it into some key themes so that you have gathered your thoughts coherently and check that you've not missed anything. Write a statement or bullet points to summarise the key themes about your ideal life as if you were living it today.

It's time to reflect on what you've discovered. There are further questions to help you do this via the website, but as a minimum I'd like you to ask at this point: if this was a description of my life, would I feel positive? Would my life feel like it had meaning? And the toughest question: if my life was how I've described it here and I died tomorrow, would I have lived it how I wanted to?

We'll return in the next Step to the importance of that last question.

Take a few moments to consider the answers to those questions, make any amendments to your outputs if needed, and then sit with them for a while, maybe a few hours or even days. This will allow you to take in how the picture you have painted feels. Try it on like a new pair of shoes if you like, walk around in them for a bit to check they fit comfortably.

When you've done that, it's time to move on to the next activity.

Practical Activities

ACTIVITY 1.2

How does my life look today?

Now that you have spent some time visualising and stating how you want your ideal life to look and maybe also stated what you don't want, it'll come as little surprise that we're going to repeat the exercise, but this time you're going to answer the same three questions based on how your life *actually* looks today.

There's a new document on the website to record your answers, if you wish to use it, so that you can compare your outputs later. The Eight Key Life Areas that you used in the first exercise remains the same, so refer to that again to ensure you leave nothing out.

My advice remains as before: give yourself some uninterrupted time to complete this activity. Be 100% truthful too; it's only by doing this that you will get the most out of the exercise and achieve results later. Remember, you are not required to share your thoughts with anyone, unless of course you choose to; this is just between you and whatever you choose to write.

Once again, there are additional prompt questions in the online document. It also has a space to summarise the themes behind your answers. If you don't use that document, write them on a piece of paper or record them electronically.

Finally, write a second statement or bullet points to summarise your observations about your current life as you are living it today.

Take some time to reflect on your outputs by asking the following questions:

- What about your current life would you like to retain in the future?
- What are you now clear that you don't like about your current life?
- What places, people, sounds or feelings would you like to eliminate or avoid going forward?

Once your outputs have settled with you, move on to the next activity.

PRACTICAL ACTIVITIES

ACTIVITY 1.3

What are the differences between my life today and my future life?

The next part of this Step is for you to undertake a gap analysis. That is, to look at the differences between the life you stated you wanted, as well as the elements you don't want, and the 'current reality' part of the life you've stated you have today. This is not about beating yourself up or looking for solutions, but it's also about not making excuses. It's about a straight up comparison . . . dispassionately for now. Think about it like doing that 'spot the difference' puzzle as a child.

Try looking at each of the Eight Key Life Areas again and use that to describe under each one what the differences are. In some areas, it may be that there are none, so state that too.

If you have differences in multiple or all eight areas, then rank the importance of each of the areas overall with regard to making change in that area. A note of caution! Do not rank them based your level of *willingness* to make change! That is something else entirely . . .

Doing this activity helps you to understand where you need to place your attention as we move forward with other exercises.

PRACTICAL ACTIVITIES

ACTIVITY 1.4

Writing a statement about your challenge(s)

The last action you're going to take, before you're ready to move forward to the next process Step, is to write down a statement about the gap you identified in the activity above. This is known as a 'problem statement' because it helps us to understand the challenge we face when making any transformation. As I said at the outset, it's part of beginning to understand the destination you're heading towards and what you're going to need to do to get there.

A problem statement should describe an undesirable gap between the current state/situation and the desired future state. It should seek to *quantify* that gap and state *why* the problem—and resolving it—is of importance.

You'll find the basic outline for a problem statement below; this will help you to set it out clearly. Further guidance is available on my website should you want it. Don't worry if you don't get your statement perfectly worded, as long as it captures the general essence of the gap between your ideal and current states, so that you know what it is that you want to be different. Just remember that the problem statement should not be defined in terms of any kind of *solution*, we'll work on those later.

- **Gap:** What is the gap—or the pain point—that exists today?
- **Timeframe, location and pattern:** When and where is the problem observed and what kind of pattern does it follow?
- **Impact:** How would you quantify the impact of the issue (cost, time, quality, personal, etc)?
- **Importance:** How important is this issue to you? How urgent?

As well as not defining the problem statement in terms of solutions (as tempting as that may be!) other pitfalls to avoid including are:

- **Symptoms:** what you are experiencing as a result of the problem, but not the problem itself. Avoid stating these here as they just confuse what the problem is.
- **Causes:** these should be examined once the problem is defined (and we'll get to these soon) as often what you think is the cause, isn't the actual cause.
- **Blame:** this process is about you, not others. As the American Naturalist, John Burroughs, said, "You can get discouraged many times, but you are not a failure until you begin to blame somebody else and stop trying".

That's Step 1 completed. I hope at this point you have more 'Awareness' than when you started.

It's time to take a bit of a breather and to give yourself some recognition for how far you've come already. You've worked hard to get to this point, so go and do something kind for *you*.

SELF STEP 1: SUMMARY

- Learnt that fulfilment is a better objective for having a life well-lived.
- Understood that fulfilment comes from people, not possessions.
- Been introduced to the Eight Key Life Areas as a framework to examine your current and future lives.
- Visualised your ideal life.
- Detailed your life as it is today.
- Conducted a gap analysis of the difference between the life you have and the life you want.
- Written a statement that outlines the key challenge that you need to address.

Not bad going, huh?

In Step 2, Direction, you'll get to work on building a connection with your desired future.

Move forward when you're ready.

"We think cag'd birds sing, when indeed they cry."
- John Webster -

SELF Step 2

DIRECTION

Direction

What is the story behind this Step?
When everything I thought was important in my life had gone and my sister told me that the world was my oyster because I had no ties and could "go anywhere and do anything", I was terrified. I didn't even know where to begin with deciding what that looked like. I didn't know how to make those choices. That was because I no longer was able to articulate what I wanted without reference to someone else: a boss, a partner, step-children, family ... basically anyone other than me.

It was when I took some time out and went on a retreat, which was, I must say, the best thing I could have done at that time, that I was fortunate to get space to think. It was there that I was encouraged to state what it was that *I* wanted my life to stand for going forward. It was a tough request, I won't lie. To place yourself at the moment where you look back across your life and ask what you see . . . now that's a sobering thought.

It's not that I had had a bad life. Far from it, there had been some amazing things that I was both grateful for and proud of. To say it had been easy, though, would most definitely have been a lie! Some of what I had been through to get to that point had been a mind-bending cluster-fuck. It's not even that I had given up along the way everything that I enjoyed, but those things I had kept doggedly doing had been tainted by the context of the life within which I was doing them. They had almost become acts of rebellion in an existence that was otherwise so constrained and compliant.

Yet, ironically, when I was granted the freedom to think about what I wanted . . . I was stumped to begin with it. No barriers and . . . my mind went blank. What did I enjoy? What might I want to try? How did I want to spend my time? What did I want to do from here so that my life meant something?

My brain went to mush. I craved freedom and then was paralysed by it. I'd grown so accustomed to hiding 'me' in the life I'd had, that stepping out into the unknown light beyond it was scary.

What I managed to write down to begin with were a few generic things:

I want to get fit. I knew that over a long period of time my body had suffered from the perpetual flood of cortisol (the stress hormone) and adrenalin (the 'fight-or-flight' hormone), borne from both my workplace pressures and toxic home environments. As I put it at the time: "I need to look after this vehicle as if it's a sports car because I have a lot of miles that I still want to do". That might not appear to be that revolutionary, but for a person who had dabbled with suicide, the fact that I wanted to now travel a lot more miles was significant.

I want to expand my social life. I had some amazing friends (I write about them frequently) but I knew that I needed to extend my network because I now had time and opportunity in my life to socialise more. What better way to do that than by doing something you enjoy at the same time? That's how I ended up joining a car club. Cars bring together such an eclectic mix of people that it's always interesting to be a part of. I might not often be able to join in with the detailed technical talk, but I do have a huge appreciation of all types of cars. I know it's not the environmentally-friendly thing to confess, but I am rather a petrol head.

I want to enjoy more live music. I've always been a massive music fan. It has been an integral part of my life for as far back as I can remember. I've sung in choirs, competitions and solo performances all over the UK since I was a child. Very much like my mum, I constantly have a song in my head that I can break into at any moment! So, seeing more live music gigs was a 'must' on my list of things I now was going to do more of. In fact, I set out with a plan to attend one live music event every month for a year. I even booked the first one whilst I was away at the retreat!

I tell you these intentions, not because they were revolutionary, but to demonstrate that they were all good starts, however mediocre they may appear . The point is your wants are your wants. It doesn't matter what anyone else thinks. I didn't set out with 'big bang' things, I began with what mattered to me. Things upon which I could build as my courage built. The fitness one, for example, has changed my life forever. Through it, I discovered boxing and have gone from hating the gym to working with a personal trainer four times a week. Anyone who knew me both before and after this time knows what an immense physical and mental transformation this has been.

I absolutely made the quote from the 1989 Kevin Costner film, Field of Dreams, my motto: "*If you build it, he will come*". It wasn't so much that I was looking for a 'he', but it became indicative of the life I wanted: that if I built that life, then the right people would be drawn to it. Friends, colleagues, business contacts and—yes, OK—maybe a new relationship one day.

All the things I chose had a real impact. Mostly because they were exactly that—things that *I* chose. There is no doubt about that. I built some awesome memories with both existing and new friends.

The blank piece of paper, as it turned out, required something more fundamental than a gym membership and concert tickets. Unsurprisingly, of course, but it took a while for me to 'get' that—several months in fact—whilst I nurtured the confidence to embrace the possibility of thinking bigger. It was actually something we had done on the retreat, which I subsequently researched, considered more deeply and developed in the weeks that followed, that sowed the seed of contemplating a different life.

I didn't heed that seed to begin with. I put back in place a replica of all the parts of my previous life and strode forward feeling more than content that I was sorted. Another spoiler: I wasn't.

Instead, something ate away at that vision because inside I knew it wasn't enough. It particularly nibbled when I started that new job I spoke of and I looked out across my future from that perspective. I realised it just held a succession of the same jobs with progressively larger remits, just as it had in the past.

What was required was a more roots and branch look at my life. To look at what I really wanted the future to include. To determine my legacy.

Bloody hell, that seemed like such an arrogant thing to say! Yet, even now, I struggle to find a different word that quite so adequately sums up why it's important that we take the gift of life and do something spectacular with it. Why shouldn't we? Why should we just be . . . average? Existing. So many people don't get a chance at life. For many they are born into a life where the odds of escaping it and into something else are stacked heavily against them. For countless others their lives are cut short before they even get going. Yet even in those circumstances—mostly *because* of those circumstances—those lives frequently have immense impact on the world around them.

I get this sounds like a speech. Preaching, maybe. A rallying cry. That's because it is! A call to action!

Life is a privilege not everyone gets. Why wouldn't you want to make that count?

If you've read 'All The Twats I Met Along The Way', then you'll know I'd stood on the precipice of death. Been pulled back from the metaphorical edge. Let me tell you that beyond the end of that book, a brush with suicide happened a second time during my recovery. So believe me when I say I know how it feels to survey your life in those final moments and see how much of it you've pissed up the wall.

And I don't mean that you have to win a Nobel Prize, invent something or cure disease. You don't need to discover a new planet or travel singlehandedly around the world. What 'legacy' means to you is personal. What matters is what matters to *you*. You enact your legacy, but only once you know what it is.

If I was going to live my own legacy, I needed to make some changes; both in what I wanted and who I was. To make that change happen, I needed to get emotional about that future.

Why is this Step important?
In the SELF Steps, this second one is called 'Direction' because here we get more definition around where you want your life path to lead to.

I love this Step because it helps you to get to the core of what matters to you. Time for the nitty gritty! Making a deep connection on an emotional level with what you want is fundamental to ensuring that you achieve it, so that's what we're going to focus on.

Once again, I'd recommend that you undertake the activities set out below when you can set aside some time to think clearly and not be disturbed for a minimum of 30 minutes at any one time. In the busy-ness of life, schedule that time in and protect it. Be observant too – catch yourself if you start making excuses to avoid facing into this stuff.

Ask: what is more important to me and those I care about than taking control of my future? Because truthfully, if you want your life to count, is anything more important? And I say that as a woman who loves to browse the internet for shoes!

One way that we can make a deep connection with the need to change (yep, I know that word is still striking a bit of fear into you, but you've gotta grab a hold on that) is to ensure we evaluate the costs to us of *not* making change. Like a balance sheet: what are our life profit and losses if we do or don't change?

The best way I have found to do this is to articulate your alternate futures. That is, to specify what your life will look like in the future, some long way from now, if you make change or don't make change. By painting a vivid picture, however uncomfortable that may be to do, you are far more likely to be motivated to start pursuing something different. Once that happens, you can look at methods to ensure those changes are successful and they stick . . . but more of that elsewhere in the SELF Steps! Oooooh, I love to tease!

You're going to do an exercise now that you may find challenging. I'm advising you of that as a reminder about taking some time out just for you and finding the best place where you won't be disturbed.

The challenge will be worth it if you want to achieve a different way of living and for that to have a dramatic, lasting impact on how you feel and what you do.

What it requires, however, is vulnerability, which is why you may not nail it in your first attempt. I understand that such brutal honesty can be hard to stomach all in one go, but that's OK; reflect for a while, and then refine or go at it again with increased understanding. You don't need to share any of your outputs from these exercises with anyone unless you choose to—this is between you and you.

Go for it and let out exactly what you feel.

PRACTICAL ACTIVITIES

ACTIVITY 2.1

My Alternate Future – Current Life

When we're born there's only one thing that is guaranteed. We'll die.

Did I mention that we are going to get emotional in this process?

Everything else that happens in between in our lives is not guaranteed or absolutely set out for us—our experiences, our choices and the people we meet all shape the intervening period—but death *is* a certainty.

Therefore, for this exercise, that is where you're going to start—with the one thing that you can rely on and be definite about.

So, the first part of this exercise involves going back to the Eight Key Life Areas that were introduced previously. Remind yourself of them now.

Have each of those areas in mind or, if you prefer, work through each one of them in turn. Either way works, just make sure you've considered all eight.

I want you to read the instructions for the activity below and then—if it is safe to do so, obviously—I need you to close your eyes for several minutes and visualise in your mind's eye the very specific scenario I ask you to conjure up.

Let's do this.

You are observing your own funeral.

How old you are. How you died. That's not the focus. What is important is that this is you at the end of your life having lived out the life you have right now. Without any changes to it.

You need to conjure in your mind where your funeral is. How it looks. Who is in the room. Bring to mind who from your current life has come to pay their respects. Acknowledge also who is missing because they are absent from your life today—that may be someone you already know or someone you would still like to have in your life, but don't.

Take yourself to that moment. Stand there in whatever setting you anticipate your funeral to be taking place and look around you. Observe the scene as an onlooker. Turn slowly through 360 degrees and silently take a thorough look around you from the spot you're standing on. You may be in amongst the gathered people. You might be standing next to your coffin. You may be hovering overhead and looking down at the scene. Wherever your vantage point; you see the scenario clearly. Think about any sounds: is there music playing? What voices can you hear? How loud or quiet is it? Breathe deeply. Are there any smells that strike you as you take in your surroundings? The scent of flowers, perhaps.

Keep that image in your mind as you continue to look around.

Then feel the emotion of it. How does it *feel* to be there? To be observing this moment? What emotions does it conjure up? Take another few deep breaths in and out and let those emotions flood through you. Don't resist them. They may include feelings of peace, panic, acceptance, sadness, regret.

Let the feelings happen, don't fight, analyse or judge them—just let them happen and notice them. Be honest about them. Welcome them. Be curious about them. Accept them.

When you're ready and have placed yourself deeply inside this experience, I want you to open your eyes. As you do so, keep those images vividly in your mind and those emotions raw within your body.

Now, you're going to write your eulogy. That is, the speech that is going to be read out as a tribute to you and your life. Remember, this is based on your life *as you live it now.* It is based upon the people, the places, the things, and your behaviours as they are today—*not* as you would like them to be. This is factual and actual, not idealised.

You can write it down or type it; there is also a template on my website that you can use that includes some prompts and questions to help.

The idea is not that this is some 'perfect' speech. It is not required to be a literary masterpiece, but it must be an accurate reflection of the life you've lived if everything in your world and about you stayed as it is today.

A few things to think about to get you started:

- Who would be reading your eulogy?
- Who would be gathered there listening to it?
- Who would be absent?
- What would be the first sentence?

Remember: no-one has inscribed on their headstone the value of their last salary payment or how much they have in their bank account or indeed anything about the possessions they own. They have words about *who* they were. That is what matters here.

Honesty, absolute honesty, is vital.

Take some time to thoughtfully complete this exercise before moving on to the next activity.

Practical Activities

ACTIVITY 2.2

My Alternate Future – Ideal Life

If you have examined the Eight Key Life Areas and are comfortable with everything you've written and feel in your eulogy about living out your life based on how it is today i.e. your 'current reality' then you probably don't need to be reading this book because you and your life is already as near perfect as it's possible to get.

For most of us, however, there is a sense of discomfort. The honesty required, the mirror it holds up to our life, and perhaps our behaviours as they are right now, can be a stark reminder that we are not living our lives as we really want them to be.

Staring unflinchingly at your own mortality and asking, "*If this was my last day on earth, would I be satisfied with who I am and what I have to show for my time here?*" can be very hard to do.

The great thing is that for as long as you *are* still here, you have every opportunity to change it . . . and that is a gift none of us should take for granted.

So, that's what we're going to work on next.

Once again, read through the guidance on the scenario you need to visualise, then close your eyes and take some time to complete the visualisation before you undertake the written activity.

35

You are observing your own funeral.

You've guessed it. You're going to imagine the same scenario, but this time, it's going to be at the end of the life you *want* to live. The life where you have been and done the things that make you fulfilled. The life where you are *Being* yourSELF in the way that is true to you.

Conjure up that image—the setting, the people present and the emotions—just as you did previously, but this time the life that is being celebrated is the one you've lived without regrets. Of course, it will be tinged with sadness—this is your funeral after all—but this time around you have made the most of whatever time you had left.

If you had lived the rest of your life, from this day forward, with no regret about the things you'd done, and no guilt about the type of person you'd been, the people who surrounded you, how would that look and feel?

Again, put yourself in that place—the sights, the sounds, the smells, the feelings—and take it all in.

When you've done that and become immersed in those images and emotions, you're going to write your eulogy a second time, again with reference to the Eight Key Life Areas.

This time it will contain what you *want* to be said about your life. A well-lived life. A fulfilled life. *Your* life.

Here are some thoughts to get you going:

- Who would be the person reading out this tribute? Now that you no longer have to conform to funeral etiquette by having the 'acceptable' person do it, who are they?

Why is it them? It might be someone currently in your life or someone you would like to have in your life.

- Who would be there because it mattered to you that they would be present at the celebration of your life?
- Who would be absent because you chose that they would be? That is, you took steps to remove their negative influence from your life.

Take your time because this version should involve some real thought. It should challenge you a bit, but also enjoy stepping into being that person you know you want to be.

Remember: focus on the things that truly matter and know that it's not about the size of your bank balance; it's about who you are.

Good luck.

PRACTICAL ACTIVITIES

ACTIVITY 2.3

Alternate future – comparison review

Now that you have the two versions of your eulogy, you need to do what you've probably already started to in your mind: examine the differences between them.

What do you observe about the two outputs? What are the key differences? Who is no longer present? What emotions do you have about each version?

This is where we go back to the idea of the 'balance sheet' of our lives. What are the credits and deficits of the life you're living today, versus the one you want? It's by understanding this that you'll make a true connection to a *desire* to change.

Do that now. Take a few moments to think about how strongly you want that second eulogy. Write down what the costs are to you personally of *not* living your life in the way that you want to. Be clear about the regrets you'll have at the end of your life if you *don't* live it in a way that is true to you.

Ensure you have a clear statement that describes why you wish to make that ideal life a reality.

SELF Step 2: Summary

In the 'Direction' Step you have:

- Learnt that being given the freedom to choose the life you want can be hard, but very rewarding.
- Discovered that facing your own mortality can be a great call to action.
- Visualised the end of your current life and connected with the thoughts and feelings that evokes.
- Visualised the end of your life as you would like it to be and understood what you want to be said about your time here.
- Written a clear statement about why making changes in your life matters to you and the costs of not doing so.

I know that thinking about your own life ending might not seem like great progress, but it is. You've faced into thinking deeply about something that most avoid. It's possibly been upsetting, but you've stuck with it because you want your life to be different in the future.

Take a few moments to feel good about what you've achieved before proceeding to the next Step.

"The fact that you aren't where you want to be should be enough motivation."

- Unknown -

SELF STEP 3

FOCUS

Focus

What is the story behind this Step?

So much of what had brought me to the place of Armageddon in my life was the repeated patterns of behaviour I'd got caught up in for years. Decades, in fact. If I wanted the new life that I had begun to imagine for myself, then I needed to think and behave differently in my future.

That, though, is a sweeping statement: Be Different. Oh! Of course! Silly me! If only I'd known that sooner! I'd have been doing it all along!

Yeah, exactly. You can't just 'be different'. Not least because not *everything* in your life or about you will need to be different. You have to understand what needs to happen to break your patterns and make some choices about how to do that. One thing is for sure though, nothing will happen if you don't know where to focus your efforts. You have to focus before you can act.

I realised in the carnage of my own life that I had to know what 'different' looked like and, more vitally, I had to break that down so that I got to the essence of the problem. If I was going to have the future that I was visualising, I needed a way to do that. It was then that I had a 'eureka' moment.

This might seem like a diversion, but trust me, it's not.

I have a Master's Degree in Lean Operations. It was the toughest thing I ever undertook academically and, in my usual fashion, I couldn't do 'just enough' to pass. I didn't even know what just enough looked like. I never had. Therefore, I gave everything to it: my time, my thoughts and (as it turned out) my health. All whilst working in a demanding job that required me to travel most weeks. I became a master (no pun intended!) of organisation, dedication and sleep-deprivation. For my efforts, I won the first ever prize that the course had awarded. I smashed it. And pretty much broke myself in the process. Which was very much one of my repeated patterns in life. I couldn't *not* give my all, whatever the cost.

Now, many people were curious why a Human Resources professional might study lean manufacturing and production techniques, especially to this depth. I'll admit that at various points, both at the time and subsequently, I've wondered quite why I had this experience in my life. Has that ever happened to you? The *"what was the point of that?"* moment? It took years for me to get an answer, but it began to uncover itself when I realised I needed to get to the bottom of what the problems/issues/challenges—whatever description or euphemism you feel comfortable with using—were that had led me repeatedly to, putting it bluntly, tolerate Twats in my life. For me, changing my approach to Twats (the one I had been and the ones I had met) was what needed to be fundamentally different.

What has the Twats I'd let into my life and a Master's in Lean Operations got to do with one another? I realised that the tools I had learnt during my studies could actually be applied to life: to personal issues as well as to physical processes. So that's what the exercises below are about: taking some of the things I'd learnt and using them in a different context. The aim of this particular tool is identical wherever it is applied: getting clarity about where solutions need to be targeted. That's why this Step is called 'Focus'.

Beyond the tool itself though, there is a wider point here. It's about how we so often have the tools we need in life to tackle what gets thrown at us. Whether it be skills, capabilities, training, or experience, we frequently ignore the transferability of them from one part of our life to another. When life chucks us a challenge, we think we cannot cope or don't know what to do. Yet, if we look across everything that already exists within us or see the attributes that were required or acquired to deal with the experiences we have already had, then suddenly our current world becomes much less daunting. Embrace the idea that you can 'lift and shift' your experiences and capabilities from one part of your life and utilise them in another. I used to see this blind spot a lot in my HR work. Where a job candidate would struggle to talk about a time they had led a team or project because they were trying to think about a work-related example, only for you to chat to them after the interview and they'd animatedly tell you how they were spending their weekends coaching the local youth football team who were successfully rising through the league table! Doh! If only they'd said that *during* the interview . . .

We'll return later to an assessment of your existing skills and experience and how to use them . . .

So, the 'Focus' Step came about because I needed, in the melee of noise in my world at that time, to find the point that I needed to start from in moving from the life I had (or, in many respects, had once had) to the one I envisioned. Where did I start with having that well-lived life? To living the life that would lead to the eulogy I wanted.

It was time for a bit of Lean.

Why is this Step important?

When you want to address the issues you might have in your life—whether a specific problem or a general unease that things just aren't working out the way you want—then it is easy to get overwhelmed by the task in front of you. You go in circles thinking about all the different facets of what needs to be done, who might be impacted and where to begin—so much so that very little might actually happen. Rumination turns into inactivity. You suffer 'analysis paralysis'.

That's what happened to me. I didn't know where to begin with sorting out the mess that my life had become, let alone understand why it had happened or the reasons that had led me to that point. Albeit that I knew it was deeper than just my most recent issues—it went much further back than that. Otherwise, why would I sit and bemoan to friends about, "*Why does this always happen to me?*". As I wrote about in 'All the Twats I Met Along The Way', I have never been about excusing the (bad) behaviours of others—that's their responsibility—but it was absolutely my responsibility to address the fact that I was letting into my life, and allowing to stay, those who treated me in a way that was less than I deserved. There was something fundamental there that I needed to address.

By breaking down those issues I ceased to see it as an amorphous mass of 'problems' and instead it became much easier to see the individual things that needed tackling—and to begin to do so systematically. That might seem like tedious navel-gazing, but I believe that asking ourselves those tough questions and facing the answers head-on is the only way that progress can be made. It's temporary pain for extremely significant long-term gain. That's what 'Focus' is all about.

I'm not ashamed to admit that I spent considerable time in therapy after my brush with suicide. I emphasise, therefore, that I'm certainly no trained psychologist or medical professional. AT ALL. I'm not advocating any of the SELF Steps as a substitute for or to circumvent any need for formal, clinical intervention. If that's what you need, then that's exactly what you should get from a licensed professional. Here, I am offering tools that help to build understanding and to pinpoint where to start in addressing issues you have in your life. These were tools I already had from my past experiences; my situation helped me to see they could be applied to my current life.

In the first two SELF Steps, you used your imagination extensively to understand what you want so that you could examine the gap between where you currently are and where you want to get to. In doing so, you've also started to make an emotional connection with the need for change.

Now, it's time to get practical. What do you *actually* need to do to enact that change? Where do you start? Let's face it, that's usually the toughest part: getting some momentum so that you can get moving. Taking that first action in forging a new path, rather than staying stuck in the same place that you currently occupy and just gazing around with uncertainty or confusion.

In the activities in this Step, you're going to get specific about where the issues are and increase your clarity about what you need to tackle. This is with the purpose of prioritising your actions for maximum impact and to minimise any feelings of being overwhelmed. I'm not promising you'll remove those feelings altogether, but small steps will feel more achievable.

It's time to dig a little further into the problem statement you wrote earlier.

PRACTICAL ACTIVITIES

ACTIVITY 3.1

Getting to the root cause of a problem

The approach you're going to use is known as the 'Fishbone Diagram'. Essentially, it is an audit of the 'who, when, what, where and how' of your life based on the problem statement you wrote in the Awareness Step.

As you go through it, you'll also be asking 'why?' so that you get to the causes of the issues.

The reason it's known as a Fishbone is because the shape is, funnily enough, like a fish skeleton, as shown in the diagram below:

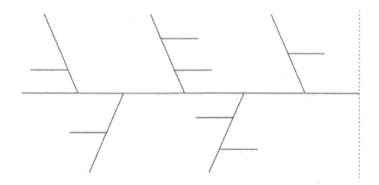

To complete yours, draw one of your own on a large piece of paper or a whiteboard if you have access to one.

At the head of the 'fish' should be your problem statement, or at least a summary of it so that you're reminded of the essence of what you're facing.

Then use each of the 'bones' of the fish to record the possible causes of the problem.

You can do this by either writing directly onto the diagram, or, as I would recommend, writing your ideas onto sticky notes (one issue per note). The latter can be useful if you wish to move them about or group them into themes later. This is especially helpful if causes fall into more than one of the categories, which is permitted. Be ruthless to avoid too much duplication, however.

The purpose of the Fishbone exercise is to brainstorm all the possible causes of the problem you have. Be mindful that they should be causes *not* symptoms. The way to ensure this is to ask: *"why does this happen?"* about each cause. You may find that you need to keep asking 'why?' in order to get to the actual cause. Accepted wisdom and experience says that you have to ask 'why?' five times before you get to the root cause, so make sure you keep going if the cause isn't immediately obvious!

Putting the causes into the categories on the diagram provides you with a structured process for reviewing those causes and understanding the contributing factors.

Keep going until you have exhausted all your thoughts and ideas. If you feel comfortable, work with someone else or share your outputs so that they can review/build on them. Only do this with someone you trust and who will be objective and not try to 'steer' your thinking based on their perspective on the matter.

When you're done, what you should have is a diagram that resembles something like this:

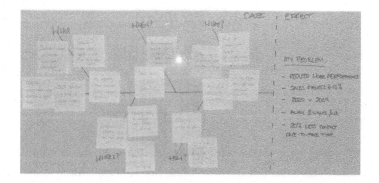

You might want to do an initial offload of ideas, but then perhaps let it sit with you for a while to see if any others come to mind in the coming hours or days. This can be a good idea because sometimes it takes a bit of time for us to get comfortable with being completely honest with ourselves about the reasons behind the problem we have.

Once you're sure you've completed this part, move on to the next activity.

PRACTICAL ACTIVITIES

ACTIVITY 3.2

Cause Prioritisation

Now to start refining what you've produced.

First, begin by eliminating any non-causes. That is, anything that you've added whilst getting all the thoughts about the issue out of your head, but that you know when you step back isn't really a contributory factor. Keep these ideas on your diagram as a reminder of your thinking by either putting a line through them or, if you've used sticky notes, placing the note to one side.

With all the items you have left, you're now going to rate them based on 'how likely' that item is to be the cause of the problem. Do this for each item by rating it as follows:

- **V** = very likely.
- **S** = somewhat likely.
- **N** = not likely to be the cause of the problem statement.

Write the relevant letter next to each item.

Next, you're going to use the same lettering system to rate each item based on 'how easy' it is to resolve that item. You should think about these ratings based on the *time* and *cost* required to resolve each of the items. For each one place the relevant letter next to it:

- **V** = very easy.
- **S** = somewhat easy.
- **N** = not easy.

Remember: challenge yourself—it won't help you if you rate any item based on how *willing* you are to tackle it! Just focus on time, costs and the resources you'd need.

Your Fishbone Diagram should now look something like this:

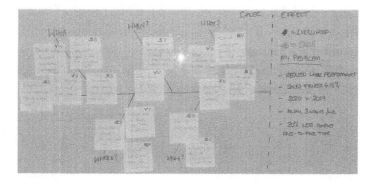

Once you've done that, rearrange or re-write those causes into a prioritised grid, such as the example that follows, starting with those that are 'very likely' to be the root cause and 'very easy' to solve.

When you've done this, you will have a visual representation of the causes of your problem and how they rank in terms of both likelihood and ease of resolution. This gives you a ready-made priority list for tackling those causes. Ta-Da!

Carolyn Hobdey

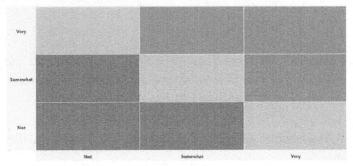

Fishbone/Causes Prioritisation Grid

Use the following grid to place your rated 'causes' into the relevant box so that you gain a prioritised action plan:

Now I don't know about you, but I feel like I need a bit of a lie down after all that! For 'lie down' read glass of wine, bubble bath, face mask, bit of a doze . . .

I'll see you on the other side of whatever treat you indulge in, and when you're ready for the next activity.

Practical Activities

ACTIVITY 3.3

Starting to plan

So, by this point in the SELF Steps you have:

- Written a problem statement.
- Uncovered the causal factors.
- Prioritised those causes.

Now it's time to begin to pull them into an action plan to work on. This action plan will evolve from this point forwards, so don't panic that you must have it all sorted at this stage; this is just the initial phase.

How do you establish good actions? How do you set them up in a way that keeps you motivated?

Setting out a plan for action isn't easy, but a good structure can really help you to think specifically about what you're going to do and by when.

When writing those actions, it is crucial that you begin to look at how you can set them up so that you will be successful in completing them. What I mean by that is that being successful at completing our actions, or even getting going with them in the first place, isn't about willpower—as much as we like to tell ourselves it is and that our inability to start or complete something is because we lack this mythical quality that others seem to be blessed with!

We will be revisiting the concept of willpower and success a little deeper later, but it's important to touch on it now as you embark on action setting for the first time here.

Bluntly, the concept of willpower is total rubbish. The reason we fail at change is not about willpower but is because we've not been specific about our actions, failed to determine the outcome we're looking to achieve and/or not created the right conditions for success. All of those take a bit of effort, but when you do them the chances of your success go up exponentially.

That's why from here forwards you're going to be given a framework for action-planning that will ensure—if you give it your attention—you succeed. It's a format for defining actions that will make sure you nail down what you want to achieve and the completion date.

This is where the SELF Steps really start to come to life; where they turn from *talking* and *thinking* about you, to *Being* yourSELF. That's the transformation that this process is built upon—to make it possible for you to turn your wants into realities. That's why the action planning process is called B.E.I.N.G. It looks like this:

- **Behaviour**: what is the action you plan to take? This is about what you're going to do that will be different from your past patterns, especially by building it into existing positive habits.
- **Explanation**: what are the specific details behind what you plan to do? This is so that you cannot let yourself off the hook by being vague!

- **Impact**: how will you measure your progress? This is about knowing when you're on and off track so that you can celebrate when warranted and course-correct quickly if required.
- **Network**: who do you need on your 'team' to help you? This is about which conversations are necessary with the people around you and being precise with them about what assistance you need.
- **Goal**: what is your deadline? This commits you to the 'when' of both starting and completing each action so that you can chart your progress towards results.

Before I let you get going with your plan, here's a few more thoughts about writing effective actions:

Keep the time-limit short
If an action needs to be completed months or even weeks from now, you'll be more likely to procrastinate and put it off. Break the achievement down into shorter-term actions and place more urgency on completing them. You'll see progress more quickly, which will keep you motivated.

Set small challenges
Don't try to change the world at once. Don't make the goal so large that you feel like you have a mountain to climb. Keep the challenge . . . well, challenging, but something that you feel is within your grasp to do. This will help maintain your enthusiasm and focus.

Score yourself
Make it a game—like a competition with yourself. Whether we admit it or not, we like the adrenalin rush of winning at something, so create small wins and then keep building on them. Can you do something faster or increase the number you do? How can you beat your own targets?

These tips will start to make your activities feel more achievable and create a sense of excitement, which helps you to commit to them more easily.

Right, now over to you. Set up a B.E.I.N.G. template—either on paper or electronically (although you might find the latter preferable because these actions will develop over the coming Steps) —to record your plan. Write some initial actions based on what you've identified the root cause(s) of your problem to be.

These don't have to be beautifully crafted actions at this stage and you certainly might not be able to complete every element of the B.E.I.N.G. structure right now. Don't worry about that, you'll keep developing these actions and filling in the constituent parts of each one throughout the coming Steps—particularly regarding timescales because these might change as the actions get shaped or new ones are added during this process. The important thing is to make a start - concentrate on getting down the 'B' headline Behaviours and actions and maybe a bit of the 'E', which is the more detailed Explanation so that you have a foundation to build upon.

SELF STEP 3: SUMMARY

In the 'Focus' Step you have:

- Learnt that, if you're serious about it, change cannot be left to chance.
- Understood that it's possible to use skills and tools from other parts of your experience to solve the issues you have today.
- Looked at all the potential root causes behind your problem statement.
- Assessed those causes so that they are prioritised.
- Started to craft your action plan in a way that sets you up for success.

This is the end of the 'Seeking' stage of the SELF Steps, so this is a good time to take stock of what you've achieved so far.

Over the last three Steps a lot has happened! Reflecting on the work you've done; you should now have greater understanding of yourself because:

- You know how you'd like your life to look today based around the Eight Key Life Areas.
- You've written a clear description of how your life looks right now.
- You've completed an assessment of the gap between those two situations.

- You've established a problem statement that summarises that gap.

Following on from that you have made an emotional connection with the need to make change in your life. You did this through examining your alternate futures, which resulted in writing:

- Your eulogy, which pays tribute to your life based on how you are living it right now.
- An alternative eulogy that pays tribute to your life based on the one you want to live.
- A comparison of the two, highlighting the differences.

Having connected emotionally with the need to change, you then began work on the practicalities of what needed to be different in your current situation to start to move towards the life you want—one of fulfilment. You did this through:

- Conducting an audit of the 'Who, What, When, Where and How?' of the circumstances surrounding your problem statement.
- Asking 'Why?' with respect to each circumstance in order to brainstorm a range of possible causes.
- Assessing each of those causes for how likely they are to be at the root of the problem and how easy they would be to resolve.
- Prioritising theses causes for the greatest ease of implementation as well as impact.
- Begun to form an action plan.

Like, go-you, right?!

Examining your life in this depth is never comfortable or straightforward. If you're going to tackle those Twats—including the one that you may have been to yourself—it's important that you take time to recognise every milestone along the way. It's totally OK if you want to high-five yourself or do a little victory dance. I would be.

Allow all your thoughts and ideas to settle. Then move forward to the next SELF stage. There, you're going to learn how to step into the 'new' you. Version 2.0, remember.

"Stand up to the bully that lives in your head."
- Carolyn Hobdey -

THE SELF STEPS – STAGE 2

SELF Expression

Expression – Who am I?

- Have you lost sight of who you are?
- Have you been treated badly by others or yourself?
- Do you want to believe more in you?

Two of the key pillars of finding meaning in our lives are storytelling and belonging, so in this stage of the SELF Steps you're going to rediscover the rich vein of your history and how to proudly claim your patch of the world.

In the busy-ness of our daily lives it's so easy to lose ourselves in the myriad roles we take on. All the demands on us, on our time and attention . . . we can quickly de-prioritise ourselves. Often until something forces us to sit up and take notice of who we are at our core.

Life events can push us into that place where we question what we stand for: finding a job, losing a job, being promoted, being made redundant, relationships (forming them or ending them), becoming a parent, losing our parents, illness . . . the list of significant life events is endless and we will all experience several of them. I've met thousands of people through my work and, believe me, I've never met any adult who has just breezed through life. Sometimes, however, wanting to change our lives is simply about how we feel about our life; that it just hasn't panned out how we imagined.

It's particularly when we hit tough times that we hear ourselves saying, "*I don't have any choice*". We can feel out of control or just plain stuck. I'm here to show you that you do have choice and you can regain control.

That's why this stage of the SELF Steps is called 'Expression'. Here, you shed your life labels and reconnect with *you*. You'll seize back control by forming a revised behavioural yardstick based on a foundation of self-trust.

The three Steps you'll go through are called 'Character', which is where you reconnect with who you are by examining the things that make up 'you'—perhaps being reminded of them for the first time in a long time. Then, by detailing all the tools and experience you already have at your disposal in the 'Trust' Step, you're going to use that knowledge as the basis upon which you're going to set some new standards—for yourself and others. You'll then know you can achieve this by detailing who you're going to be going forwards, which is what will happen during the final Step of this stage, 'Boundaries'.

"You cannot love someone you don't know."
- Brownwell Landrum -

SELF Step 4

CHARACTER

Character

What is the story behind this Step?
I've mentioned previously my tendency to people-please. It had started in my childhood and carried on right the way through to my forties. My efforts to 'be nicer', in an attempt to be loved, had merely resulted in a series of scenarios where I wasn't loved for who I was, because I didn't really *know* who I was. As I constantly bent myself out of shape for each new relationship—be it personal, friendship or work—then how could I possibly expect anyone else to know me enough to care either? Of course, I didn't know this at the time.

#idiot

When everything subsequently dropped away from my life, I had to start all over again. Gone were the things that I thought made up 'me' and I was left questioning what I stood for. Who am I?

What I wasn't, was those labels. I suddenly realised that they are, in most cases, transient. You move jobs, people come and go from your life for a variety of reasons and material things are . . . well, just things.

I learnt that last one the hard way. I grabbed hold of all the belongings from the home I'd occupied with my partner, in the hope that these tangible reminders of the wreckage of my life might provide something firm to cling on to. They didn't. They went into storage because I had nowhere else to keep them and I didn't see most of them for another year— some of them I still haven't. Apart from a few sentimental keepsakes, I didn't miss any of it. None of it made a difference to how stable or otherwise I felt. None of it helped me get my life back on track any sooner or made me feel better about what had happened. Instead, they hung around in my conscious mind like the relics of a past life that they actually were. Like a museum exhibit of All The Twats I'd Met Along The Way . . .

Instead, I had to set about working out who I was *without* all those things. Without the labels and artefacts that had previously provided an illusion of my identity. In hindsight, which is always such a powerful experience, I'm enormously grateful for that moment when everything caved in. The chance of the reset of me. The alternative was that I carried on bumbling through life being everything that anyone wanted of me. I'd possibly never have learnt what my best friend meant when she'd said numerous times, "*you need to learn to love yourself*". I hadn't had a clue up until then what she meant or where to start with doing that. Whilst I'd loved often, I'd never loved me.

OK, I'll admit I'd have appreciated not reaching the point of needing to rediscover myself in quite such a dramatic

Carolyn Hobdey

fashion, but the fact that it happened changed everything for me—literally everything—about how I felt about me and my life. Don't confuse that with the fact that everything about me had to change—that's not the case. Large parts of who I fundamentally was remained. I just had to unearth them again and alter my relationship with how I felt about them. It's also not to say that I haven't tripped over and fallen flat on my face a few times since. I really have and I will share that with you! But rarely is a change process linear and smooth—that's why we perceive it as hard. It is a challenge. Yet, even if the journey is a bit zig-zaggy or up and down along the way, you can still reach the place you're aiming for if you know what that place is.

Part of what I had to understand when it came to my character, was that I had *value*—to myself and others. It was the one feeling, belief and certainty that had eluded me all my life. I began to see it, though, when friends and family stepped forward to support me. I learnt it even more in one simple sentence from one of those friends, "*You forget that I get so much from our time together too*". All along I'd been thinking our relationship was entirely one-sided. That she was only helping *me*. In that moment, it suddenly struck me that this was reciprocal. She valued me! That this was not one-way traffic or selfless on the part of these people. Others sought my time, my friendship, my opinion and counsel.

I began to listen to their reasons why; their words and actions. Tuning into that was a revelation. I wasn't a hopeless, lost cause after all.

Why is this Step important?

Whilst this Step might look like a short one (and, let's face it, you hoped that would mean it was easy, right?), that's only because the activities here involve sending you off into the world (wide web) to do some exploring.

That's because this Step is all about YOU: who you are and what you stand for. Helping you to reconnect with what is important to you and learning why.

What I mean by this is that we take on roles and labels in life that help us categorise and find a sense of belonging—all of which can be really positive—but they also risk hijacking who we are and, particularly, the person we thought we would be when we imagined our future.

Being someone's partner, parent, boss, employee, friend, sibling—all the potential roles that help structure and define our lives—are not who we really are. Frequently, we lose sight of this.

That's why it's time to focus on you. To take an unflinching, in-depth look into who you are at your core and to reconnect you with that person. I'm going to ask you to be selfish with your attention (because I'd hazard a guess that you rarely are) and embark on a journey of discovery. The reason for this is because you can only start to build your life and take charge of who surrounds you, when you know yourself first.

The activities below are designed to do that. None of them are about referencing the roles you play in other people's lives. They are about what brings you meaning and motivation, as well as what your behavioural standards are. Some things you may already know—in which case, you'll find them a helpful reminder—whilst others are likely to provide new insights. Either way, the tools here are about gathering data and collating it in one place so that you gain a holistic view of you. From there, you'll be able to make informed choices and decisions in subsequent Steps that ensure the life you have is far more attuned to your authentic self.

PRACTICAL ACTIVITIES

ACTIVITY 4.1

Below are links to various expert questionnaires. Complete these exercises by typing the links to the external web pages into your preferred internet browser.

All these questionnaires are free to complete, although some sites require you to create a user account to access them.

As with any of these types of assessments, they are designed to be a guide and not provide 'absolute' answers.

What are my *Values*?
The Demartini Value Determination Process:
www.drdemartini.com/values

What gives me *Energy*?
The Five Institute Vitality Test:
www.fiveinstitute.com/the-vitality-test

What is my *Personality*?
The Keirsey Personality Types Test: www.kiersey.com

What *Motivates* me?
www.psychologies.co.uk/tests/what-motivates-you.html

Print, save or screenshot the results of each one you complete so that you can refer to them in the next activity.

PRACTICAL ACTIVITIES

ACTIVITY 4.2

From the questionnaires you have completed, summarise the key outputs/findings for each into a statement:

- **My Values are:**

- **My Energy comes from:**

- **My Personality can be described as:**

- **I am Motivated by:**

Yes, there were only two activities for you to complete here, but did you see what I did? I got you to do five things in the process. Sneaky, huh? What I'm expecting is that you now have lots of insights with which you can move forward onto the other Steps in Expression.

SELF Step 4: Summary

In the 'Character' Step you have:

- Learnt that you need to listen out for signs about how others value you—both through their words and actions.
- Understood that your 'life labels' don't define or tell you who you are.
- Completed various questionnaires to gain insights about your character.
- Summarised those findings into a number of key statements about you.

"Who you are is defined by what you're willing to struggle for."
- Mark Manson -

SELF Step 5

TRUST

Trust

What is the story behind this Step?
One of the biggest things I realised I had lost, as life had taken its various swings at me, was trust. Trust in others, for sure. There had, as you already know, been many Twats I had met along the way that I now needed to rid my life of. Yet, it was more severe than that. I had lost all trust in me. In fact, it had been gone for a long time, which had made my personal life, in particular, a self-perpetuating cycle of bad calls.

I didn't trust my own judgement—especially about intimate relationships—or my ability to make key decisions. The lens through which I viewed everything suddenly came from a place of self-doubt and suspicion. How was this [*insert: choice/decision/person*] going to turn into my next failure?

I began to do what so many of us do when self-doubt has taken up residency in our heads: I sought the counsel of *everybody*. I was trying to look for answers to my issues in everyone else—particularly because the wise words of friends, family and even fairly casual acquaintances seemed to carry much more weight than anything I could determine for myself. This was different to what I said in the last Step about listening to others. By that, I meant to hear their positive feedback about you. To understand that you have value to them as much as they do to you. What I am referring to in this Step is listening to everyone else's opinion about what to *do* and never trusting your own.

At one time, I was consumed with so much worry that I was at risk of making no decisions at all. As someone wise once said to me, "*It's better to make a wrong decision, than no decision*". How true that is. The alternative is to stay stuck and, at that point in my life, that was not an option or luxury I had.

There was nothing for it. I had to re-build that trust. It had to start with me. I'd long since learned that those that don't trust themselves cannot trust others because they inherently come from a place of thinking everyone else is as untrustworthy as them. I'd been there. I'd been that person. When I'd been unfaithful in my marriage it made me think everyone was a cheat. Changing that view of myself was explicitly why I had entered my last relationship with the firm promise to myself that I never wanted to be that woman again. That's not to judge anyone who is; I have done it myself and know there are myriad reasons why those things happen in relationships, hence why I am not about to start preaching to the contrary. I'm just saying that at that stage being faithful—and, therefore, trustworthy—was a decision I made that was right for me. As an aside, the irony was that whilst I was a bastion of virtue in that relationship, he left me having found my replacement whilst we were still together. But, hey ho, I was able to exit with a clear conscience at least!

Anyway, the point that I want to make is that trusting others starts with self-trust.

When faced with what felt, at the time, like the worst set of circumstances I had ever experienced, there was no guidebook to help me find my way through it. I had to rely on what I had and start from where I found myself. In the desolate days and nights (there were a lot of sleepless nights!) when I had time to think about what had happened, I began to put together the pieces of what needed to be done to alter my circumstances. Ultimately, I was responsible for sorting this mess out. I had to find the belief that I *could*.

There was nothing that anyone could 'tell' me that would re-ignite my faith in myself—although one fantastic friend was great at giving me regular perspective about how far I had progressed. I had to find it. The only way to do that, I realised, was to reference all the things I had been through in the past and what they had taught me. All the skills I needed were, in fact, already in place. I had them.

Now, I didn't have some 'a-ha' moment that made me realise that was that case. Rather, it was a slow and painful process of digging myself out of a hole that meant that the insight I speak of came much later. That's why I can share it with you now. The reality was that I started to draw on my organisation skills, my ability to communicate well, the network of people I knew, the influencing capabilities from my work—and so the list went on. Yes, the context was different. Yes, there was a lot to deal with all at once, so I was pulling those skills out willy-nilly without much thought.

Yet, I absolutely had already got everything that it was going to take to turn the situation around. For some parts, I needed to access my professional skills—where in some pretty awful scenarios at work it had been necessary to be dispassionate and detached to deal with a difficult person or problem. That's not to say I was devoid of emotion when that happened, but it had been necessary in my work to place them to one side to get through whatever the business or an individual had needed me to resolve. I'd been both formally trained and had gained experience for such eventualities.

In other parts, I needed to draw on my previous personal life. I'd been through heartbreak and I knew all about grief or loss in their various forms. I'd experienced them and I was still here to tell the tale. I needed to remind myself that I had what it took to get through it; that the pain would, in time, pass.

Most significantly, I learnt about trust through gratitude: the practice of looking for something good in every day. Any chink of light in the darkness, from birdsong to a tasty meal to a smile from a stranger to acknowledging something good that I had done. The accumulation of these many tiny micro-moments of 'good' has an amazing impact on your mental health. Through them, I learnt to trust that there was still positivity in the world and good in me, despite any sadness I currently felt.

What I gained trust in overall was my ability to just get through 'stuff'. That there was indeed an 'other side' that would eventually be reached. That the world kept turning and mine would too. Nothing stays the same forever, not least our emotions.

Knowing this was what allowed me to love again.

Why is this Step important?

One of the most pointless things we can be told is, *"you just need to be more confident."* Whether it's about our ability to meet new people, deliver a project, take up a new hobby, or speak in public. I hate it when people say that. If only it was that easy!

What we gain confidence from are our abilities—whether that's skills, experience or achievements. By this I don't mean winning awards and studying for university degrees, but all the small stuff we have learnt and accumulated as knowledge throughout our lives so far. That's what makes up our strengths and capabilities.

When we are assured of our competence, then we gain confidence. Making small changes, consistently making them, and growing our capabilities alongside; that builds confidence.

Confidence is made up of several elements, which is why in various guises it runs throughout numerous of the SELF Steps, rather than being a Step of its own. Here, it's important to reference its relationship to competence—in that reminding ourselves of what we know and can already do provides a self-assurance that is vital when making change.

You're going to continue the self-discovery that you have already started in the previous Step. This will be done by conducting a full audit of your skills and experiences. It is important to document these in addition to the external data you've gained from the Character Step questionnaires so that you have a rounded view of all the things you are *already* capable of, in addition to the qualities you possess.

This isn't just about academic qualifications and courses you've attended (although these should be acknowledged and recorded too), it's also about the things you've been through—good and bad—that have developed your knowledge and ability to deal with all things 'life'.

Sometimes, you simply need that reminder. To take a moment to reflect on and recognise how far you've come. To explicitly see what you've been through, coped with, overcome and succeeded at, as well as what it has taught you along the way; especially in the toughest times. In the life events we encounter there are so many transferrable skills that we frequently take for granted as we reach the next hurdle. Here is where you pause for a while and take notice of those.

As I'm heard often to say, *"If you're not your own biggest cheerleader, no-one else is going to step up and shake their pompoms for you"*.

So, what are you waiting for? Start waving them!

"Happiness will never come to those who fail to appreciate what they already have."

- Buddha -

PRACTICAL ACTIVITIES

ACTIVITY 5.1

Skills audit

Conducting an audit of your skills helps to bring back to the fore all those things that you have learnt or trained in throughout your life—whether it's to do with work, hobbies or homelife. You might want to refer back to the Eight Key Life Areas document as a prompt about the different areas of your life where those skills might have been cultivated.

Then, detail them under the following headings:

- Training provider (if known).
- Course or workshop title.
- Summary content.
- Key learning points.

Take a moment to review your outputs and give yourself credit for all you've learnt.

PRACTICAL ACTIVITIES

ACTIVITY 5.2

Experience record

So many of the experiences you will have had in your life help you to develop capabilities that enable you to deal with other situations, which is why it is useful to be reminded of what those experiences were and what they taught you.

Do that by completing the following for each notable experience—big or small—in your life:

- What was the situation?
- How did it develop you?
- Summarise the skills and competences gained.

Read back through your experiences and appreciate what you are already capable of.

PRACTICAL ACTIVITIES

ACTIVITY 5.3

Practicing gratitude

Steadily building a fan-following over recent years, gratitude is defined as, 'thankful appreciation for what an individual receives, whether tangible or intangible' (Harvard Health, 2021). The practice has gained a reputation for:

- Developing resilience.
- Creating positive emotions.
- Helping to handle adversity.
- Relishing good experiences.
- Connecting people.
- Improving mental health.
- Managing anxiety/increasing calm.

Therefore, getting into a practice of regular gratitude helps us to build positivity within ourselves and the world around us. With positivity comes the belief that you can deal with the bad days as well as the good. Positivity builds self-trust.

There are numerous ways that you can practice gratitude, but regularity is key. It takes about 66 days to create a new habit, so that is how long I would like you to keep a Gratitude Diary for. To do this you only need a notebook or some paper and a pen. It might be tempting to record it electronically, but I want to dissuade you from doing that because the physical act of writing things down enhances the impact with gratitude.

Each day for the next 66, write down anything you are grateful for. Anything at all, whether it's the beauty of leaves on the trees, birdsong, the smile of a stranger, someone who lets you in front of them in a queue or that extra sprinkle of chocolate that the Barista puts on your cappuccino.

There is no lower or upper limit on how much or what you write about. All you need to do is write about what you are thankful for each day and remember that no-one will read it other than you, so let your thoughts and feelings run free.

Do this every day and observe how it impacts your mood: you may just develop a happy habit for life!

SELF Step 5: Summary

In the 'Trust' Step you have:

- Learnt that trusting others begins with trusting yourself.
- Understood that appreciating your competence is a key component to improving your confidence.
- Completed an audit of the skills you have developed in your life.
- Made a record of all your key experiences and what they have taught you.
- Started a daily practice of gratitude to cultivate positivity.

Having a plan is good. Sometimes having a plan 'B' is not. Now, before we leave 'Trust', I want to say a few words about micro-cheating. *"What is that?!"*, I hear you cry. Well, micro-cheating is those small acts of infidelity that don't involve you being fully unfaithful. For example, they could be flirty texts to someone other than your partner. It could be where you have what I would call a 'plan B' person in your life—someone who would be a back-up option as an intimate partner if things don't work out with your current one. It could be knowing who your go-to person would be if you wanted some 'fun' and to let off some steam without strings attached. It might be staying in touch with your ex and not telling them that you're now with someone else, just in case. Recognise any of that?

I have said before, I am not here to judge. I'll openly admit that I have done all those things at points in my life.

For me, I was desperate to be loved and awful at exiting the poor relationships I allowed myself to get into. So, my 'plan B' behaviours were about getting attention (not love, even though I wanted it to be that) when I wasn't getting what I needed from my actual partner.

Why I raise it here is that, if this is you—and it's OK if you're cringing a little—I want to encourage you to have a think about these behaviours. What do you do and—most importantly—*why*? What need, emotion or void are you satisfying by doing this? What cost is there to you of doing it? Consider whether it is serving you well and reflects the person you want to be. Were those 'plan B' people turning up to hear that alternative eulogy you wrote—the one where the words were all about the excellent life you've lived?

Your answers matter here, not anyone else's opinion.

"The only people who get upset about you setting boundaries are the ones who were benefiting from you having none."
- tinybuddha.com -

SELF Step 6

BOUNDARIES

Bouudaries

What is the story behind this Step?

Classically for a people pleaser, I struggled with boundaries. I wanted to be loved and it led me to do, say and tolerate things that were some distance below the standards that I should have had for myself.

That's where the story behind this Step begins: I didn't really have a standard. Not one that I was conscious of, at least. I'd make perpetual excuses for others' behaviours and frequently my own in response. It came back to not knowing who I was and what mattered to me. It was founded in the fact that I didn't think *I* mattered. I placed no value on myself and, therefore, I couldn't draw a line that demonstrated where my standards began or what the distinction was between that and the unacceptable.

I would return repeatedly to the scenes of 'crimes': toxic relationships, in particular, were my metaphorical drug of choice. I would continue to be certain that if *I* changed, if *I* were better, if *I* did what 'he' wanted, then this time it would last. This would be my first last love.

I have worked hard to address and eliminate feelings of shame in my life, yet my previous lack of boundaries is the one place where I must be especially vigilant against shame creeping in. Not least it rears itself here because I feel the need to tell you that I wasn't a slut. I wasn't having sex with lots of different men. I would have sex with the same one over a long period of time or, instead, would not be having sex with someone, but would be engaged in some other ill-advised 'situationship' encounter. Frequently, I was baffled about how these even came about! Either way, what I was doing was unhealthy. Even though, compared to conversations with others, I would say that my 'body count' is pretty damn low. Yet, why should I even feel the need to justify myself? Would it make me less of a valuable human being if I'd slept with dozens of men? As a woman in our current society, I have to say that I believe the answer to that is still, sadly, 'yes'. Whilst the needle of judgement has moved over the preceding decades, it remains stubbornly so that women are treated differently (negatively) to men in this regard. That judgement comes from all sides—women judge other women as much as, if not more than—men do on this matter. As such, there remains a stubborn amount of shame around sex for women due to the huge disparity between how we view men's sexual activity versus women's. I could properly get on my soap box about it, but I'm going to save it for another book (that I already have planned!) beyond this Twats Trilogy.

I attempt to be kinder about my shame these days by reminding myself that we are all human. We make mistakes and do stupid stuff. We're complex creatures who are frequently very simple in thought and action. I wanted to be loved because I believed I never would be and it made me needy, foolish and reckless, both within intimate relationships and friendships.

It's important to me that I give you examples of this so that I honour the searing honesty that I began with when I wrote 'All The Twats I Met Along The Way'. It was then, and remains, vital that I shine a light into the dark corners of life and our minds so that we minimise shame and maximise the chance for people to speak up about their own lives. That is fundamental to my purpose in being a writer and commentator.

So here goes . . .

I had an affair with my boss. Those who have read my first book of the 'Twats Trilogy' will remember 'Brad'. Needless to say, I'd not advise this as a good idea. In fact, I had various indiscretions at work, but those are stories for the third book of the Trilogy: 'Twats at Work'.

I was wooed, and cruelly used, by my personal trainer, let's call him Gluteus Maximus. I was just on the road out from my recovery from the incidents of 2018 and I hired a trainer for the first time. I was vulnerable, to say the least, and—as it turned out—completely naive to what I now understand goes on in that world. The fact that I succumbed to this cliché makes me cringe, even more so that I absolutely did not believe that it was that cliché at the time. I must stress, this is not my current trainer—he's lovely. In fact, I spend so much time with him I call him my 'Gym Husband' and, as we all know, most married couples don't have sex! I made myself laugh then.

My serial offence has been second chances. I'd messed up numerous parts of my own life, so I was always ready to give someone another chance. The benefit of the doubt. An opportunity to learn and be better. That's what I'd say about them all. What I was really doing was ignoring the red flags that these people were waving right in front of my face. I'd spent my life learning to 'be nicer', so I swatted those flags to one side and believed that I could be that good person who helped somebody else to improve. I could fix them.

And there it is. My Achilles heel. As a dear friend once said to me, *"When you're a smart woman you look for a project to occupy you"*. Goodness me, was that true! I liked a doer-upper. Someone who was broken that I could 'save'. Call it what you will. Misguided. Arrogant. An unmet maternal instinct. Deluded. A challenge. The need to be needed. It was probably a bit of all of those.

Some of my most useful examples occurred around the same time. The first was my initial dating experience after the end of the relationship that led me to reset myself and rethink my life. Yet the cautionary tale extends further than that.

I've said before that I was busy putting back in place all the accepted tenets of success in my life—new job, new home, new car—you know the drill. The final part was to start dating again. Now, I know that you might instantly say that I wasn't over my previous relationship. I have to say, that whilst what he'd done had undoubtedly left scars, still being in love with him was not the case. The way that he had behaved and the fact that he had morphed beyond recognition into somebody else in order to snare (sorry, I should probably say "woo", but he was definitely a 'snare' kind of guy) his new love meant that I had very rapidly fallen out of love with him. Honestly, I really had. As the quote elsewhere in this book says, *"You can't love someone you don't know."* That was absolutely true for him. The issue, instead, was that I hadn't finished healing myself. That was true in respect to other areas of that relationship as well as all the feelings I'd had about myself over the years prior—the feelings that had led me to that most recent toxic relationship.

So, there I was back on the dating scene. I was ready to love someone else, I just hadn't finished learning how to love myself.

That's how the next Twats I encountered found their way in. In through that little chink of hope I held that my 'one' was still out there to make me whole. Now, please don't think I've since become a cynic and don't believe in love and happily ever afters, I truly do, but at that time I expected them to arrive in my life to rescue me. More than that, I imagined a man would complete me.

It's why, when one particular guy showered me with intense attention through online dating, I quickly became swept along. Let's call him, Aphrodite, because his real name was feminine and he liked to think he was a bit of a god . . . he was anything but. Why am I specifically calling him out? For the reason that he exemplified so much of what women experience when dating and that I hear lamented all the time: avoidant, unavailable, game-players. Worst still, those that either don't know or won't admit what they're like or that they're doing it. They truly believe and seek, instead, to present themselves as 'good guys'. There was always some fairly plausible, heartfelt, 'please feel sorry for me' reason why he couldn't commit to the relationship at any particular time. Only to show up again, lighting up my phone about two weeks later, expecting to pick up where he left off by love-bombing me all over again. What I realised, finally, was that he likely had a harem of ladies whom he would operate on rotation, with no intention of committing to any of them. The sport was merely to get you to the point of wanting him again. Truth was, he was cruel, contrary and a commitment-phobe. The worst kind of player. He blew hot and cold with a pattern that it took me a while to acknowledge, but which was so predictable you could almost set your watch by it. It makes me cringe now to think I fell for it more than once, yet satisfied that in the end I got the chance to call him out on it.

Then there were those that would disappear for even longer periods of time and then re-emerge out of nowhere, but talk to you as if they've never been away . . . And what is it about married guys thinking they can come onto you when you're a single woman?! But that's a *whole* other topic for a *whole* other bottle of wine! Anyway, I'm not going to even attempt to solve the mysteries of the male mind or dating behaviours here—that's yet another book! The point, instead, is that when my anxiety levels about the unavailable, avoidant, arrogant and—let's be blunt—arsehole-type men that I was *still* allowing to take away who I was, had reached fever pitch, I made a significant decision. For all the work I had already done on myself at that stage, I realised that I was trying to take on too much (I can feel my best friend rolling her eyes with familiarity at this point!) by trying to bring someone else into the still-growing phase of my recovery.

That's when I decided that I was going to spend 12 months man-free. They were proving to be a distraction from all the numerous great things I had going on in my life. There was so much to be positive and grateful for that the perpetual disappointment of their behaviour was magnified as a rather large fly in my otherwise sweet-smelling ointment. More than anything else though, it was time to admit that I just wasn't strong enough to hold all my boundaries firm all at once. My love life had long been my weak point and, whilst I was making progress by getting back out dating and saying 'no' to some undesirables, the fundamental issue remained that I wasn't quite 'there' yet with my self-love to allow me to bring in someone else to love—I was too ready to trade the former for the latter.

OK, so you could accuse *me* of avoidance; that my decision was just putting off the problem. Maybe, but you have to remember that I had in its place created a new boundary that I had to hold firm to—not get into a relationship with anyone for 12 months. And I can tell you, I stuck true to that. Yes, early on, whilst the plan settled in, I went on a couple of dates. I snogged someone. OK, so I'm human. But beyond that and, for the remainder of the term, I was a fully paid-up celibate singleton.

What my stories here have in common is something really vital to what the SELF Steps and my entire philosophy is all about. That is, that we need to see our transformation as a series of Steps—not a quantum leap. The setting of my standard and the communication of those boundaries across my life was, as I said, the hardest part of change for me. Unsurprisingly, therefore, these examples are of where I fell off the wagon after my initial transformative phase. And therein lies the lesson: our progress and change are constant. It is a repeated series of being the *current* best version of yourself, not an end result, not if you truly want to have a well-lived life.

Indeed, when I talk about boundaries here, I must emphasise that I don't just mean sexual ones. I'm talking about all types of unacceptable behaviour in relationships, whether they be friendships, intimate relationships, familial, associates or colleagues. The need for—and breach of—boundaries exist everywhere. Including with ourselves, I realised.

What I hadn't yet grasped was that when it comes to love, there is no cavalry. You love you. Period. That's where it starts from and where it ends. Only when you love *you* can you love anyone else, and they can love you back.

Why is this Step important?
Unless we know our standards and set firm boundaries by which we live our lives, then we will always be at risk at being taken advantage of, poorly treated and being cruel to ourselves in the process. If you want a different life you need to start as you mean to go on. That's not to say, as I have clearly demonstrated, that it is always easy to stick to these standards initially—they will get challenged and frequently so—and you will trip over them for sure. Yet, the more you're reminded of them and why they matter to you, then the stronger your resolve will become. Then, as you apply them you will begin to feel better. I promise. Yes, there are going to be times when their application is uncomfortable, but when you know that

it's right in the longer-term and the release from your life of the toxicity that regularly accompanies someone or something that breaches your standard, you will start to feel the benefits. They will be huge.

What is key is that you have to look out for your *own* red flags. That is, the behaviours you demonstrate when you're *not* setting or sticking to your own boundaries. My best friend says, for example, that she hears my standards dropping every time I say, "*I do get it that . . .*" or "*I understand why . . .*" and then proceed to make an excuse for someone else's bad behaviour.

It kills me to admit it, but she is right. Always.

These days, when I say that kind of stuff, she immediately asks, "*And how does that sit with your standard?*". I cringe with recognition every time such that it has become my mission to not be in a position where I utter those fateful words! We all need a friend who loves us enough to hold us to account like that. We'll talk more about those friends in Step 7, 'Connection'.

PRACTICAL ACTIVITIES

ACTIVITY 6.1

Who is in your network?

To understand where the boundaries need to be in your life, you need to examine your network. The first activity, therefore, is to compile a list of all the people in your life. People in your family, your friendship groups, your work associates (if applicable), from the hobbies you do . . . You get the idea.

Again, return to the Eight Key Life Areas to help you put some structure around the gathering of this list. There is no right or wrong number of people in any area, or overall. It's just you making a list in any of the relevant categories of the people that reside there in your life. Using that as a table, put down whatever names come to mind from your circle, before proceeding to the next Step.

For this activity, there is a table template on the website for you to use.

PRACTICAL ACTIVITIES

ACTIVITY 6.2

Who is key?

Having identified all these people and placed them into each life area, I now want you to identify the *key* people. By that, I mean the ones that have the greatest *impact*. They may, or may not, be the ones you have contact with most often—for example an immediate family member that you live some distance from—but the ones that have the most significance and influence on your thoughts, feelings and decisions in a particular part of your life. Who crops up the most in your mind or in real life?

Do this by highlighting them in your list and then state *why* you consider them to be 'key'—how do they impact you?

PRACTICAL ACTIVITIES

ACTIVITY 6.3

What is your value?

In this next exercise I want you to take each of the Key People you've identified in the previous activity and, in turn, next to them record the answer to this question:

If you were to meet and ask each of them what value *you* bring to *them*/their world, what would they say?

Don't overthink it or second guess it. Go with your immediate instinct and write that down.

When you're done, take a step back to review your answers and appreciate for a moment the positive impact you have on others and how.

PRACTICAL ACTIVITIES

ACTIVITY 6.4

Who are you going to be?

If you're going to live your life on your terms and make that ideal eulogy a reality, you have to be clear about what those terms are: who are you going to be, starting from today?

So, surprise, surprise, the next exercise in this Step involves you doing just that: stating who you are and taking ownership for stepping into the shoes of being that person. So, let's make them a gorgeous pair, huh?

By doing this you have the best chance possible of living without regret and also of staying on course with that plan when life—and often the people you encounter—try to take you off track.

The way you're going to do this, is to write what I call a 'Character Commitment'. Essentially, this is a statement that is deeply meaningful to you; it sets out who you intend to be going forward and how you're going to approach life. Essentially, write down your answer to the question:

Who am I going to be, starting from today?

How you go about writing it is up to you.

You could write something in each of the Eight Key Life Areas about who and how you're going to be.

You could structure it under each of the SELF areas (Seeking, Expression, Love, Fulfilment).

99

You could speak from the heart and write it freestyle.

If you want a template that you can use with some prompt questions to assist you, then you can find one on my website. Remember though, that this is a very personal 'manifesto' for your life, so you don't need to follow the template exactly if that doesn't work for you; it's just a guide.

I'd suggest writing down what immediately feels right having done all the previous activities until this point, and then leaving it for a while for the contents to 'settle' with you. Go back later and refine it if you wish. However, don't lose the initial raw essence of your emotions and passion.

Where you keep your finished Character Commitment is up to you. Keep it to yourself, show it to someone, store it on your phone to reference, print it out and put it somewhere where you'll be reminded of it daily.

Whatever you choose to do, it should be a document that you keep coming back to. Remember, you're committing to making change, so it's likely that you will find yourself in situations where you'll need to be reminded of the commitment you've made to yourself. Knowing and owning who you are and regularly recalling the path that it places you on, is a really great way of ensuring that you get the life you want, not the one that others expect of you.

SELF STEP 6: SUMMARY

In the 'Boundaries' Step you have:

- Learnt that setting standards and boundaries starts with you.
- Compiled a list of all the people in your network.
- Identified who amongst them is 'key' in your life.
- Understood why you are of value to those key people.
- Written a Character Commitment stating who you're going to be starting from today.
- Ensured you're going to live in accordance with the eulogy you wrote for your ideal life.

*"I used to think that the worst thing
in life was to end up alone.
It's not.
The worst thing in life is to end up with
people who make you feel alone."*
- Robin Williams -

THE SELF STEPS – STAGE 3

SELF
Love

Love – How am I?

In the first two stages of the SELF Steps, your focus has been on understanding who you are, what you stand for and what you want the legacy of your life to be.

Now it's time to explore further another essential component of our lives: other people.

We've already begun to list who is in your sphere, but now you're going to get more specific about their impact on you. I must advise you, some of this might get uncomfortable. That's because it is necessary to confront some truths about who and what you've been tolerating. Also, perhaps about what's been missing in your life. These are each equivalent hurts that we may have chosen to live with. Maybe they are not conscious choices, but they may be painful choices, nonetheless.

The 'Love' stage of the SELF model requires some fortitude. Yet, I want to remind you here that all the Steps you have been through up until this point are designed to provide the firm foundation of self-knowledge and belief that you need to now deal with those people external to you. Having the right people around you is essential to you having the right life, because only by having the freedom to be unapologetically you can you truly find Fulfilment; the final stage of the SELF model.

In this third stage you'll examine who is in your network (Step 7: Connection), look at making decisions about those people by confirming that you have all the tools required to give you Courage (Step 8) going forwards, and finally increase your understanding of how to handle the necessary conversations with each of them (Step 9: Compassion).

You can tell a lot about a person by the company they keep, so make sure yours says things about you that you are proud of.

*"Make sure everybody in your boat is rowing
and not drilling holes when you're not looking."*
- Brownwell Landrum -

SELF STEP 7

CONNECTION

Connection

What is the story behind this Step?
I've said previously that the one thing that astounded me when I was in the depths of despair in my life, was the people who stepped forward to help me. This was underlined during the 2020/21 Coronavirus pandemic, when I was contacted by so many people who wanted to check I was OK whilst I spent large swathes of lockdown on my own. Indeed, the pandemic taught us all about the value of Connection. The human touch that we abruptly lost—even contact with strangers in the supermarket, coffee shops or on the daily commute—was a stark reminder of how we are, inherently, pack animals. As I've said previously, being in a group has long since been the foundation of human survival, so to be separated from those groups was bound to be destabilising.

Yet, there will also have been people that we didn't miss. Just as there were people who vanished into thin air when they knew my life had fallen apart—like they might somehow become infected by whatever malaise had caused everything to crumble. Those people were notable by their absence.

What this period of my life taught me was the immense power of my network. Greater still, was the realisation that I wasn't alone. Each of the people that came to my aid—emotionally, practically, physically—showed me that we need to be part of a tribe long after our forefathers had ceased to roam the Savannah or protect each other from actual predators.

I came to see that there are a variety of people that are needed in our lives, each playing different 'characters' in order to ensure that our network is complete. I didn't have, or need, all these skills or characteristics in one person. In fact, that is impossible. Instead, I needed different things at different times and they came in the form of different members of my group. There were times when I most definitely needed the wise counsel of the friend who was adept at steering me towards what I needed to do next when I was totally overwhelmed and simply couldn't work that out for myself. They weren't there to show me the 'big picture' because that wasn't their skillset, but the right next step, they were perfect for that. Then there was the person who showed up to physically sort through and organise the chattels of my life. They were not the person who was going to help me plan my future, but they were wonderful at seeing the practical task immediately in front of us and getting stuck in to completing it. Then there was someone who would just make me laugh and show me some light-heartedness in the darkness, the one who insisted on taking me out for food and drinks and, in the process, taking me out of my head, even just for a little while. The list went on.

Prior to this moment I had seen my network of friends and acquaintances as exactly that, a group of people. Sure, if you'd pushed me, I could have talked about them as individuals and the role that they might play in any one particular friendship group. What this dramatic time in my life did, however, was provide me with a perspective through which I was able to view them very differently and start to see the parts they played in forming a complete team around me of exactly what I needed to get through what I faced.

It made me realise that this team/tribe/group/clan/crew—call it whatever you like—were essential elements of a network that we should all seek to build. Many of you will already have parts of it in place, but likely won't ever have assessed it. Others may never have thought about it at all. My greatest wish for myself was that I had seen and known which person was which 'character' *before* my world gave way, it would have made for a more efficient route to understanding where I needed to turn at what moment for the right support.

Then there is the flip side. Some people are negative influences in our lives. Tough to say, but true. They might be people you've chosen to have there: friends, partners, employees. They might be those about whom you feel you have less choice about their presence—family members, work colleagues, other members of clubs or societies you belong to. Either way, these are the people that make you feel a bit 'meh'.

Mood Hoovers.

Energy Vampires.

Drains.

Fun sponges.

There are various names for them, but the impact they have on you is the same. Others are just downright cruel.

In the pursuit of a life of *Being* unapologetically yourSELF, these ones need special attention. That's the challenging part. Don't panic, though, I'm here to walk you through it bit-by-bit and, I promise you, you will feel better for making some decisions about these people. More of that in Step 8: Courage.

The reason I know this, is that I discovered that in learning to love myself, in administering self-care, in discovering that I had to prioritise me if I was to have the life I'd described for myself, then there were some people that I just needed to let go. They weren't 'my people' and, most likely, I wasn't theirs either. Remember, I was a people-pleaser and I wanted to be loved/not be left alone in life—so it was hard for me to cut people loose or minimise their impact when leaving them behind wasn't an option.

For anyone who has read my book, Redefining SELFISH, which is the introductory model to the deeper-dive concept of *Being* yourSELF that you're discovering here, you'll recognise already the concept that I introduce in that text about 'Elimination'; the idea of getting rid of the things and people that detract from our lives. I learnt this the hard way and I continue to have to tackle it to this day. I was notorious for letting the wrong people in and take up residence in my life, I still do occasionally, but these days it doesn't last because I have seen, felt and experienced the positive transformational power that comes from stepping away from these people. Short term pain? Yes. But the relief and freedom that comes afterwards is well worth it.

Why is this Step important?
In all honesty, I developed the tools and exercises in this Step because of suicide. I've shared that I had a brush with death in the immediate aftermath of the disaster that my life became mid-way through 2018, but I have spoken less often about how, 12 months later, it happened again. I was devastated. I had done so much work, put key aspects of my life back in place and had been helped by so many people, but what I'd done is pick myself up and carry on almost as if the intervening 'blip' hadn't happened. What I hadn't done at that time was process all the aspects of what I had gone through, nor fully realise the twelve elements of the SELF Steps.

This time, however, when the internal cloud of suicide began to mushroom within me once again, I instinctively knew I had several people to whom I could turn. As I backed away from the edge of the railway platform and stood against the wall letting its solid, cold form hold me steady, waiting for my breathing to do the same, I thought about the people on my 'team'. I knew I wasn't alone and I was reminded that there were people around me—genuine people—who would not be freaked out by me sharing how I was currently feeling. They would, instead, stand alongside me, hold my hand if necessary, and walk with me through to the other side. To safety.

I knew then that, subconsciously, I had gathered my top team in my head. I had learnt who they each were, what character part they played in my network, and under what circumstances I would reach out to each of them. All I had needed was a way to record this that meant I had clarity in the good times so that I could just implement it during the bad. Forewarned is forearmed and all that.

So, for me, this process started off as suicide prevention. So much of what we hear in the devastating aftermath of someone taking their own life, are the tributes from friends, family and colleagues about how much they were loved and not alone. I wanted to design a constructive way for every person to review the people around them so that they knew they were not alone either—because the truth is, none of us are, however we live our lives. Yes, there might be gaps in your network—you may not currently have every character type you'd appreciate in your team—but knowing that allows for decisive action to address it. This is why I designed the 'Top Team' tool. It's a way of assessing the key people in your network and then making informed decisions about them based on what role they perform in your team and their impact on you. Each character has possible positive and negative behavioural implications, but by evaluating the key people in your life against these you can keep close to you the right ones and distance the wrong ones.

There are 12 character types, which are detailed in the table below:

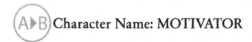 **Character Name: MOTIVATOR**

Description: This person naturally has lots of energy. They are a 'go-getter' who encourages you to adopt the same approach. Being practical and goal-oriented, they have their own life-plan and inspire you to do the same. They put you on a path forward and accept no excuses.

In their positive state: Energetic. Encouraging.
Goal-oriented.
In their negative state: Pushy. Bull-dozer. Unsympathetic.

 Character Name: FINANCIER

Description: Great with numbers, either through education or experience, this person ensures your finances are in order. Naturally cautious in their approach, their guidance will be based on logic and reason; they make well thought-through decisions.
In their positive state: Financially astute. Cautious. Logical.
In their negative state: Dispassionate. Risk-averse.
Single-minded.

 Character Name: CHEERLEADER

Description: The person in this role will bring lots of enthusiasm based on their deep belief in you and your ability. Accepting you for who you are, they behave like they are your number one fan. They are there to celebrate your successes and pick you up when you fall.
In their positive state: Enthusiastic. Positive.
Non-judgemental.
In their negative state: Subjective. Wearisome. Unrealistic.

 Character Name: CHALLENGER

Description: Given that they hold the mirror up to your behaviour, sometimes this person can be the one that makes

you feel uncomfortable. Their honesty provides perspective
and has the potential to raise your standard.
In their positive state: Objective. Honest. Principled.
In their negative state: Harsh. Critical. Judgemental.

 Character Name: HELPER

Description: With their can-do attitude this person is not
afraid of getting stuck in and doing hard work to help you
to get things done. They are not daunted by a practical
challenge and are very task-oriented.
In their positive state: Practical. Hard-working. Finishes
the task.
In their negative state: Blunt. 'Does' rather than thinks.
Short-termist.

 Character Name: CONNECTOR

Description: Being well networked, this person knows
people who know people. They will invariably have someone
they can put you in contact with to assist with whatever
challenge you face. Often, they see opportunities for
connection where others don't.
In their positive state: Opportunistic. Networked. Strategic.
In their negative state: Wheeler-dealer. Manipulative. Self-serving.

 Character Name: ENTERTAINER

Description: Always at the centre of a good time, this
person's light-hearted approach to life can create an upbeat

mood. They are fun and humorous; not much gets them down and they can be a welcome distraction from life's tougher times.

In their positive state: Fun. Light-hearted. Clown.
In their negative state: Frivolous. Leads you astray. Undisciplined.

 Character Name: MENTOR

Description: As a considered thinker, this person guides you to finding solutions through signposting to options or offering an alternative perspective. This is based upon their innate ability to see the bigger picture and to help you do the same.

In their positive state: Perspective. Thought-provoking. Solution-oriented.
In their negative state: Unyielding. Impractical. Talking, not doing.

 Character Name: CREATOR

Description: This person is full of ideas and adept at creative solutions. They paint a vivid picture of their vision and hence encourage you to imagine many possibilities or take a longer-term view.

In their positive state: Visionary. Positive. Future-oriented.
In their negative state: Dreamer. Impractical. Strategic only.

Character Name: PROTECTOR

Description: With an inherent desire to shield you from harm, this person will step in to help you or even take the lead when they perceive that this is what is needed. Looking to provide a haven for you they are keen to relieve you of your burden.

In their positive state: Safety. Caring. Parental.

In their negative state: Over-protective. Interferes. Worrier.

 Character Name: COMFORTER

Description: Providing solace when you need it, this person is a great listener. They show kindness, will support you when needed, and are someone you go to when you want to press pause on your world for a little while.

In their positive state: Listener. Quiet. Peaceful.

In their negative state: Overly cautious. Maintains the status quo. Unchallenging.

 Character Name: ADVISER

Description: Always ready with practical advice, this natural problem-solver will bring logic and an unemotional assessment to your issues. Especially good at helping you to resolve immediate, short-term dilemmas they will often be a specialist in a particular field of expertise.

In their positive state: Logical. Tactical. Specialist.

In their negative state: Limited foresight. Emotionally detached. Uncompromising.

In the activities of the last Step, you listed out all the people in your life and identified those that you considered to be key. That is, those that you feel have the greatest significance, impact or influence—whether that's practically or emotionally.

In the activities that follow, you're going to look deeper at those key people and your relationship with them. This helps you to understand who you have around you and how they impact you. It examines what that does to support or sabotage your sense of fulfilment and in achieving the life you really want or being able to live as the person you want to be.

Our network is vital in our lives. It is scientifically proven that relationships—social interaction—keep us healthy and more positive. They protect our brains as well as our bodies. However, it isn't how many friends or contacts we have or even being in an intimate relationship that makes the difference, it is the *quality* of those connections. What's particularly interesting is that when scientists have examined what defines a quality relationship, it's the ones where you feel you are able to count on the other person when times are tough.

That's why, in these next activities, you're going to look at each of your key people and consider what role they play in your life, and—perhaps the toughest question—the extent to which their impact is positive or otherwise.

Once again, this requires absolutely honesty. Only by taking the time to assess the people around you and doing that, dare I say, dispassionately, can you understand the influence that's having on you. Think about:

- Who is consistently showing up for you, but you're perhaps not recognising their efforts?
- Who has a tendency to take you off in the wrong direction?
- Who threatens to capsize you altogether?

It's time to take a look . . .

"The person who tries to keep everyone happy
often ends up feeling the loneliest."
- Unknown -

Practical Activities

ACTIVITY 7.1

Which characters do you have around you?

For this exercise, you're returning to the list of key people in each of the Eight Key Life Area categories.

The task is to identify the character type that each of these key people play in your life using the earlier table.

When you choose a character type for each key person, remember that this should be the *primary* role that they play, whilst acknowledging that for some they may dip into other roles on occasion too.

There is no need to place someone into *every* character type if you don't currently have them in your network. Conversely, you can have multiple people in the *same* character type. There are no right or wrong outputs—just see it as information to help you to look at the people you have around you.

Place your list into their character types before progressing to the next activity.

"Your best outputs come from your most honest inputs."
- Carolyn Hobdey -

PRACTICAL ACTIVITIES

ACTIVITY 7.2

What impact do key people have on you?

Now that you have identified the role that each of the key people plays in your life by identifying their primary character type, it's time to assess the impact they each have on you.

This is where you place them on a grid based on two factors.

The first is the impact they have on you on a scale where there is 'joyful' at one end and 'toxic' at the other; this is placed on the horizontal axis.

The second, vertical axis, is to assess the frequency of contact: how often or otherwise do you have contact with this person? That 'contact' could be on any form: face-to-face, telephone, online or in your thoughts/decisions. It's an assessment of how often they are 'with' you in some form, be that physically, mentally or emotionally.

You should draw a grid that looks like the one over the page.

For each key person I first want you to place them onto the grid based on where they sit *today* by marking their position with an 'X' and placing their name or initials next to it. Refer to the earlier table to assist you with considering the positive and negative behaviours that each character type displays. Think about how the person leaves you feeling *the majority of the time* after you have interacted with them.

I appreciate that there is a challenge in doing this. It's going to require a level of truthfulness that may be uncomfortable. Just remember, this isn't about how much someone loves or cares about you, nor does it mean that you don't love them if you say that currently their impact on you is negative.

The aim is to make an objective assessment and gather data from which you can subsequently make choices and decisions.

Next, I want you to position each person a second time onto the grid based on where you want them to be *in the future*. Do this by marking their position with an 'O' and placing their name or initials next to it. For some, their position may not change, but mark them on again to show this.

When you have finished, you should have a grid that includes all the key people you identified in Step 6 with an 'X' (current impact) and an 'O' (future/desired impact) for each one.

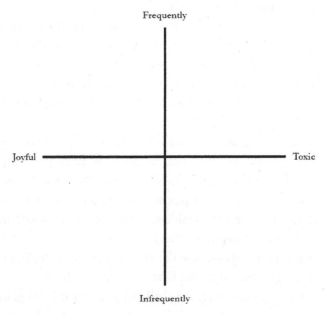

PRACTICAL ACTIVITIES

ACTIVITY 7.3

What choices do you need to make?

Placing each person onto the grid by making an assessment of their current impact on you and again based on their future, desired impact, should lead to some choices about what to do next.

To assist you with these, below are some options dependent upon whether the person currently (those marked with an 'X') falls into a 'Joyful' or a 'Toxic' area of the grid.

For each choice you make about what to do about that person, refer to the corresponding question set and write down your answers.

Before you do that, let me explain what a 'key conversation' is.

Key conversations
Change is rarely a solitary activity.

When you change something about you or your life, it's likely to have some knock-on impact on those around you. That might be a positive impact or a negative one depending on the situation you find yourself in.

Invariably, when you set about making change, especially when that change is focused on making your life the best it can be—living on your terms to achieve what fulfilment means to you—then there will be people that you need to talk to about that.

That may be because you need their help to take the steps you want to or to ensure you stick to your plan. The change may impact them or your relationship with them. They might need to learn some new things about you; how you feel or your desires for the future, for example. It may be that informing them is just the right and decent thing to do.

Often when we make changes we've spent some time thinking about that, so how we start to share those thoughts with others needs some consideration; that's what key conversations are all about.

Key conversations are where you plan what you need to say, to whom and how. It involves thinking about the other person's perspective and, in particular, any objections they may have and how you might handle those. It considers where and when the discussion might take place—if you have the option to determine that—for the greatest success. Key conversations also are focused on creating a 'safe' environment for all parties in the discussion to make it as productive as possible.

I'll return in the next Step to concentrate on how to increase the likelihood of a productive conversation.

Joyful/Toxic choices

- **Set A**

Choice:
Live with it/I'm happy as it is (i.e. do nothing).

Questions:

What are the consequences—positive and negative—of not taking any action with this person?

Where am I making excuses to not take action and why might that be?

- **Set B**

Choice:

Increase/decrease* frequency of contact through my actions. (* Specify which)

Questions:

What behaviours will I actively change in order to make this happen?

When will I start to make this change?

- **Set C**

Choice:

Hold a key conversation with this person.

Questions:

What is the outcome I want from this conversation?

What are the key points that I need to say to this person?

Some of these questions involve you making decisions about what specific actions to take next with each person.

It is worth reinforcing here that deciding to do *nothing* is in itself a decision. I'm not looking for you to take action in every case, or indeed to plan actions that you currently don't feel are possible or appropriate based on your current emotions or situation. Even where someone may be having a negative impact on you, it might not be right for you to do anything about that straight away—what you do and when you do it is entirely *your* choice. All I ask is that you:

- Consider what might be possible straight away—there are always choices, even when there seem to be none!
- Fully understand the cost of not taking action where someone is having a negative influence on you.
- Question why you're choosing not to take action: is it genuinely unwise or is it because it is just 'difficult' to do? If it's the latter, we have strategies coming up to help you with that!

SELF Step 7: Summary

In the 'Connection' Step you have:

- Learnt that it is important to think carefully about the people you surround yourself with.
- Discovered that there are 12 character types you're going to identify.
- Assessed what character types you have around you.
- Understood what key conversations are.
- Identified what impact the members of your network have on you.
- Made decisions about what action—if any—you're going to take in respect of each person and why.

"What you accept when the cement is wet is what you get when the cement is set."
- Carolyn Hobdey -

SELF STEP 8: COURAGE

COURAGE

Courage

What is the story behind this Step?

For so much of my life I'd had a mixed relationship with confidence. I had seemed a paradox, even to myself. I suffered years of low self-worth and yet I would take on ever-greater challenges and push myself regularly outside of my comfort zone: bigger jobs, travel, study, moving to a new location. Yet the two were, in fact, inextricably linked. I drove myself to do those things that might appear like they required confidence exactly *because* my self-worth was so low. I needed to be better, always. To prove myself. To try and be perfect in order to be loved.

Self-belief and confidence are essential for having a well-lived life. It's why I like Lewis Howes' confidence equation. If you've not seen it before, it goes like this:

Congruence + Competence + Connection = Confidence

All three elements were things that I had done—mostly inadvertently—during my own transformation, which is why you will find them all, overtly or otherwise, somewhere within the SELF Steps.

Yet, when it comes to beginning to enact the things you need to do to bring the SELF Steps alive for *you*, then it's going to take more than confidence, it's going to require Courage.

My personal requirement for courage stemmed from the need to let go of the 'wrong' people in my life. For you, it may be something entirely different that you find daunting: you want to transform your life, leave a legacy, just be more positive in the day-to-day. The point being that you already have all the ingredients you need to feel confident. The SELF Steps are there to show you that you do and to provide direction about how to focus your efforts to utilise your skills.

Yet, whatever your reason for doing these exercises, I'm guessing that part of why you picked the book up was something about the concept of De-Twatting your life that resonated with you. Yeah, I'm not sure if that's a real word either, but we kinda get what it means, right?

For my part, I had struggled with relationships in my life in two ways due to my low self-worth and poor self-confidence:

1. I wasn't good at instigating friendships because I feared rejection.
2. I got into and stuck with the wrong intimate relationships because I was afraid I'd end up alone in life (I'm like a broken record about that one, I know, but it was huge in my life for a long time!).

Tackling these habitual behaviours was where *I* needed courage.

That's why in the Courage Step we look to make decisions about the key people in your life—especially the toxic ones. The intention is to plan practical actions based on the assessments you conducted in the previous exercises. I knew that I needed to make myself face into some truths about the people around me if I was going to have a better/healthier/ happier/fulfilled life going forward. That wasn't easy, these were long-standing, deeply ingrained behaviours that I was changing. It's the very reason I needed a process. That might sound clinical in the face of human relationships, but it was the only way I was going to be able to hold myself to account for making and sticking to a decision, even if, as you'll discover in the activities at the end of this Step, that decision was to do nothing. Yes, I'm reinforcing that point here: a decision to do nothing about a person is still a decision. What matters is that it becomes a *conscious* decision and that you have fully thought through the consequences to you of doing nothing.

You see, my naturally glass-half-full/it'll-all-be-OK outlook on life was great in many ways, but it led me to see upsides when I should have been seeing the dark sides of several people. I trusted where I shouldn't have done and made excuses for others where they were not deserving of such grace. They were being Twats and I let them get away with it. I didn't think I deserved better and so I was, therefore, being a Twat to myself by letting it continue.

Finding the courage to let people go from my life—friends, partners, employees, tradespeople— (you name it, I was unilaterally too kind in all areas of my life!) was fundamental to me having a better life.

What I learnt was that when I did, the overriding emotion was . . . relief.

Yes, there was some hurt, some sense of loss. Yet, it was when these people had gone—the calls, the texting, the 'drama' of it usually—that I realised what a weight they had been in my life. I had given so much of my time and energy to getting involved with them—again, my 'bad' because I was frequently trying to resolve/fix/help them, which usually wasn't helpful to me—that it was only when I put this baggage down that I could see how heavy it had been. Slowing me down, diverting me and taking up brain space that I should have been putting into other, more productive things.

I'd be lying if I said I didn't miss some of them because in certain cases and in a few respects, I do. There are times when a memory is aroused that makes me think about them fondly and I want to pick up the phone and say, "*Do you remember when . . .?*", but it is swiftly followed by the memory of why I have left them behind. The moment of wanting to contact them quickly passes as the pain of their loss is replaced with the reminder of the greater pain their presence brought. The dictionary definition of courage is '*strength in the face of pain or grief*' (Oxford Languages) and so letting these people go, Dear Reader, is Courage in action.

Why is this Step important?
Finding the courage to do the things we find most difficult is hard, especially when it comes to relationships. The fear of losing those relationships stops us from having the

conversations we need to, even if losing them is the right thing for us!

Yet, here's the thing: the more we step forward into the difficult stuff, the more courageous we become. Why? Because frequently before we do difficult things, we imagine them to be far worse than they actually turn out to be. Our ego catastrophises situations to prevent us from entering into them, in an effort to keep us safe from what it perceives as 'harm'. That's why we have to do our best to stand back and weigh up a situation objectively: asking ourselves what it is that we *actually* fear. What's the worst that could happen? Really? When you ask yourself—and, most notably, your ego—that question, frequently the answer is a bit . . . embarrassing. Pathetic even. Because it's often nothing that would be that bad. Someone will say "*no*" perhaps. Maybe they will laugh at you. You'll lose from your life someone who isn't meant for you—whether that's a friend or a partner, even a family member. Yet, when you weigh up all the things that might go wrong against what you stand to gain from being courageous, then it might just become a no-brainer that you should just go for it. So what if you get knocked back? So what if someone turns out not to be your kind of person? You know, those people that deride you for trying something, are those very people who would *never* have the courage to do what you're doing—that's why they want to keep you small; it makes them feel better about their small life. Believe me, you'll never encounter criticism from those that are doing brave stuff in their own lives.

Making decisions about who you have around you and who, bluntly, you're going to let go, can make an enormous difference to the quality of your life. The sense of relief felt when you no longer carry the burden of how they influence your feelings is huge. In finding the courage to take action consider this also: how might you be making them feel in return? If they are negative towards you, what is it that you do or say that might bring that out in them? It's possible that you bring out the worst in each other. I'm not saying your actions are intentional, but it just might be that your impact isn't what you intend. Consider that you letting them go or reducing your time with them, might just be the best and kindest thing you do for *them*. One of you needs to muster the courage to make the break, for the good of both of you. Why shouldn't it be you? You'll come away feeling remarkably positive about doing the right, mature, brave thing. For demonstrating Courage.

PRACTICAL ACTIVITIES

ACTIVITY 8.1

Who gets to be part of your Top Team?

You've gathered a lot of information and done plenty of thinking about you and the people that are around you in your life. That's because our vibe attracts our tribe, remember, and who we have around us is an incredible influence on the life we have, both good and bad.

This activity is about selecting your 'Top Team', that's why I like to refer to it as getting a seat at your table. Whether you see it as a dinner table, a boardroom table or around your kitchen table with a cuppa: who would be those people that you would gather?

There is one seat at your table for each character type. That's not to say that there aren't other people you have in your network who fulfil the same Character role, but this is about selecting the principal one. *The* one. Together, these are your closest network of people upon whom you can rely.

Now, you don't have to love spending time with all of them. You don't have to imagine that you would actually get them together all at once because they would enjoy each other's company either. You just have to be confident that each one is the right person to occupy their place because you trust them—they are your go-to person for that role. They are the people that walk alongside you and don't leave when times are tough. They are the people you feel you can call upon in difficult times. I also refer to them as your '3am people' because they're the ones who you could call in the early hours if you were in trouble and they'd be willing to help! They are also the ones who will want to celebrate with you when you make progress.

If someone doesn't meet these criteria, they don't earn a seat. Simple.

Similarly, you may find that there are empty seats at your table at this stage. This may be because you don't have anyone in your life of a particular character type or because those that you have are not suitable for or worthy of that Top Team seat—either because they currently sit in a toxic zone on your impact grid, or they are not someone in whom you yet have sufficient trust.

That's OK. Part of the actions you'll need to take subsequently will be about addressing this situation. If you have seats to fill, you need to be proactive about how you're going to either cultivate an existing connection to bring them closer into your trusted team or find a new connection over time that will take that place.

Draw a rectangle on a piece of paper. This is your 'table'. Place a circle at one end (this is your seat) and then 12 other circles around it—six on either of the two long sides—like in the diagram opposite.

Put your name in the circle at the head of the table. Label the other 12 circles for each of the character types.

Place in the relevant 'seat' the name or initials of the key person who will fulfil that role in your Top Team.

If you have gaps in your team, put the word 'vacancy' next to the relevant circle.

If you have potential candidates for any of the character types, but whom are not yet right to take one of the seats, write their name and which role they might take elsewhere on the sheet so that you are reminded of who they are.

This is your Top Team. Sit back and contemplate it for a moment. How does it make you feel?

PRACTICAL ACTIVITIES

ACTIVITY 8.2
Taking action about people

Now that you have made a number of assessments and gained insights regarding you, your life, and the people in your network, it's time to begin the process of action planning about the steps you're going to take to make changes.

There may be actions about people that you want to spend more time with or increase their positive influence in your life. There may be a decision about actions you need to take regarding a more negative influence or a plan to minimise the impact they have on you. You might plan to achieve this either through strategies to change your own mindset and response to them, or by physically distancing from them. There may be actions you need to take about *you* to achieve the life you articulated you want—the one that brings you fulfilment.

Whatever the actions are, you'll need a plan otherwise you'll forget them, avoid them or not complete them. Structure—even if that doesn't seem very sexy—is key to holding yourself to account.

Here, it's time to start putting in place that structure as you work towards *Being* yourSELF. With that in mind, you're going to continue building that action plan you started earlier. As a reminder, it has the following components for each action you need to take:

- **B**

Behaviour: What is the overarching action you need to take?

- **E**

Explanation: What specifically are the details behind that action?

- **I**

Impact: How will the outcome look or success be measured?

- **N**

Network: Who will you need to help you, involve or speak to?

- **G**

Goal: When will you start and complete the action?

Over the coming Steps you'll keep developing this action plan, but here start to write down your actions regarding your network and Top Team outputs. This involves primarily filling in the 'B' element of your B.E.I.N.G. action plan template. Complete as much as you can of the other sections too. Think about who and what you need to attend to. In what order and by when might you need to address them? Hold yourself to account and know that it will be worth the effort to get the right team around you.

SELF Step 8: Summary

In the 'Courage' Step you have:

- Learnt that having the life you want relies upon having the right people around you.
- Understood that Courage grows the more we do things that scare us.
- Decided who gets a seat in your Top Team and why.
- Identified where the gaps are in your Top Team and what you need to do to address them.
- Considered what action you need to take regarding your Top Team and others in your life.
- Continued populating your B.E.I.N.G. action plan.

"If you want others to be happy, practice compassion.
If you want to be happy, practice compassion."
- Dalai Lama -

SELF Step 9

Compassion

What is the story behind this Step?
I'd like to think that in my life I have shown a lot of compassion for others. I'll admit, sometimes too much and for longer than some of them deserved.

Where I had failed—spectacularly—was with self-compassion; the ability to think and act kindly towards myself had frequently eluded me and I was, as I've shared, incredibly hard on myself in my own head.

No doubt, the Character Commitment that you wrote earlier included words about how you want to be treated by others and how you want them to feel like you treat them well too. I'm certain that the eulogy you wrote based upon the future life you want to have, contained words spoken about the type of person you have been. A good person. Kind. Thoughtful. A positive influence in others' lives.

That why Step 9 of the SELF Steps is about Compassion because both inward-focused and outward-facing compassion are needed in order for anyone to show up in this world as the best version of themselves.

When it comes to inward-focused compassion it's important here that you consider your relationship with failure. Undoubtedly, there will be times when you're making changes to you and your life when it won't go right. A decision you make or a course of action, maybe you 'fall off the wagon' of your behavioural standards—you break that diet, you don't go to the gym, you avoid a tough conversation with someone, you have sex with the wrong person—whatever the reason you fall short of what you set out to do or be, you need to be kind about why that happens. That's not to say that you let yourself off the hook for repeated failures on the same things—when that happens it requires attention about why and some corrective decisions—but a temporary blip in 'performance' should be seen as exactly that.

For me, when it came to not falling for the charm of . . . well, Twats, that's where I was at greatest risk. I had to understand that I was breaking decades worth of habits and it wasn't going to be a switch I could flick to have the problem solved overnight. I got a bit better at spotting them. Sometimes I didn't. I became stronger at removing them when I realised what they were. Sometimes I didn't. In general, the trajectory was positive, and I had learnt to consult with and listen to the views of friends in the process of understanding when the actions of others were questionable. I got it wrong at times— one notable instance in particular, but he's a tale for another time—yet, the fact that I also had examples of where I *was* now doing the right thing, well that was progress in itself. I didn't get involved with some of the wrong men who were in the wrong situation in their own lives, who tried to instigate or re-instigate a relationship of some sort with me. Those who disappeared without communicating, I gave up chasing them. When it came to online dating, I tried to be as kind as possible whilst also being honest and ensuring I moved on quickly when someone wasn't for me, which was really about being honest with myself.

Learning self-compassion was hard. Putting myself first was hard. What I learnt, however, was that I grew stronger with each difficult conversation or decision. Realising that my new boundaries were most frequently challenged by those who stood to gain the most by them not existing. Like the guy online who asked me to send an explicit photo of myself within the first few texts and, when I refused, told me that I, *"need to understand that with online dating you need to exploit your assets"*. To which I replied, *"I am. My greatest asset is my behavioural standard for myself."*

Mic drop

Despite a few of these kinds of idiots reaching us—and, even then, there isn't a need to be cruel—for the most part we need also to have external-facing compassion. There were times when the transformation I was making made others feel uncomfortable. One accused me of being *"brain-washed"* by the things I was learning. Another said that the things that were contributing to me redefining who I was and the life I wanted were *"like a cult"*. These comments hurt and frustrated me, in the moment it made me feel like those people didn't want what was best for me. When those emotions passed, however, I came to a more rational place of understanding. For them, this was scary. What they had known and relied upon about me was shifting and they were having to adjust too. They were also having to do that without the benefit of being inside my head. They hadn't had the opportunity of processing what was happening for me or of having gone through the experiences and learning that I'd had the privilege of being exposed to. They were playing catch-up with what was happening for me, and I realised that I needed to show compassion for that.

All the choices and changes I was making meant that I had to have some well-considered conversations. Some of those were ones where it was necessary for me to make myself vulnerable by asking for help, offering myself up as a new friend or telling someone I was interested in a relationship, for example. Others were more challenging conversations about how someone else's behaviour impacted me, decisions I was making about my future that others might find hard to understand, or why I would be distancing myself from them if they were not a supporter of the new standards I was trying to put in place.

I had to have each one of those conversations and they all required compassion. The compassion to know it was the right thing for me and communicating with good intent for them.

I needed a plan.

"Be good to people.
You will be remembered more for kindness
than any level of success you could possibly attain."
- Mandy Hale -

Why is this Step important?

It may seem hard to plan for conversations because you cannot account for what the other person will say or anticipate how they will react. It's why we all frequently leave things to chance, perhaps having had a quick run through in our heads or taking the classic 'hoping for the best' approach. We hope that, when it comes down to it, the other person will have our thoughts magically transmitted to them via osmosis or telepathy and they'll just 'get it'. Better still, perhaps we won't be required to say anything at all. For anyone who has read my book, Redefining SELFISH, you'll know that I write in there about a concept known as the 'Illusion of Transparency'; where we just expect others to know our thoughts and feelings without the need for us to say anything. We do it all the time, but when you think about it it's nonsense!

Conversely, the other route we take is that we think that because we're human beings and we communicate all the time, then we'll just innately be able to convey what we want to without much effort; we talk all the time, right?! You'll find the right words. You speak the same language. They'll understand you, for sure! It'll all be *fine*.

Both approaches are naive and fraught with issues, of course.

It's why the Compassion Step is here. To ensure you make some plans about the conversations you intend to have. *Need* to have.

Planning for these discussions might seem a bit of a pain, but if you want the right outcome—for you and them—forethought is essential. Not least because being respectful to others and ensuring you remain firm in your intent are both central tenets of your new standards and your success in achieving the life you want: a well-lived life. The one where you are *Being* unapologetically yourSELF.

Planning these conversations doesn't require courage, it requires a bit of time. Having the conversations may require courage, but you will gain that if you plan.

Who is with you on your new adventure and who is not will all come down to how well you manage these conversations.

That part is down to you.

PRACTICAL ACTIVITIES

ACTIVITY 9.1

What conversations do you need to have?

Look again at the outputs from your impact assessment of the key people around you and also the seating plan for your Top Team.

It's time to plan the conversations you're going to need to have. Ask the following questions:

- Who are these conversations with?
- Why is each conversation important?
- What may be challenging about them?
- What are the key points you want to get across?
- What outcome are you hoping for?
- Where and when is the best time to have each conversation?
- What order might you need to have them in?

It's important here to consider also who is missing from your life or your 12 character types. What 'vacancies' do you have? Do you have someone in your network of key people for that might be a suitable candidate for that role in the future? Ask:

- What is the gap that needs to be filled?
- Why is it important to my success in living a fulfilled life that the gap gets filled?
- Do I know the right person to fill it? (e.g. are they in my network, but just not in my close network right now?)
- If I do, what is the conversation with them that I need to plan for?
- If I don't know the right person, who do I already know that can I speak to in order to find them?

Develop any new actions that are needed and add as much of the detail behind them to your B.E.I.N.G. action plan.

PRACTICAL ACTIVITIES

ACTIVITY 9.2

How can you plan for constructive conversations?

We've all experienced times where, despite what we believe to be our best attempts, a key conversation that we've had with someone—either at home or at work—hasn't turned out as we intended. In fact, I'm sure you've had times when you wished you hadn't even bothered because you feel like you have made a situation worse!

These experiences have a tendency to put us off from having the conversations that we need to, with the result that we either avoid that conversation altogether or put it off to the last possible moment; this frequently has an even greater negative impact on the success of that interaction.

The good news is that it is possible to improve your skills in having those key conversations—it isn't a matter of innate ability that some people are just fortunate enough to possess.

To understand how to have more effective conversations, it's useful to understand why they don't go well in the first place. This can change your mindset about believing that you're either not good at it or that it must be the other person's lack of ability to communicate with you.

The main, overarching reason why key conversations don't go well is a matter of safety. That is, any number of the parties involved in the conversation feel that their position is 'unsafe' in some way. They might feel afraid, attacked/got at, disrespected or misunderstood, for example. These unsafe feelings drive a reaction. These reactions are deep, primal instincts formed over thousands of years. First the reaction is physiological (raised heart rate, increased adrenalin, reduced cognitive processes—i.e. the ability to think straight), which is what we characterise as the 'Fight or Flight' response.

Next comes a behavioural response. This may present itself in a variety of ways, but the two underlying reactions are known as either 'violence', which can show itself through physical or verbal aggression (being controlling, stereotyping, name-calling, shouting, lashing out), or 'silence', which is withdrawing from the conversation either through clamming up (completely or partially) or actually physically leaving the conversation (avoidance).

When we start to understand that creating safety is the foundation stone of having a good conversation, we can start to look for times when either we feel unsafe or someone else in the conversation does. From there, you can learn techniques to handle that and return the situation to a position of safety.

I describe this as there being four things 'mis-sing' when a key conversation becomes unsafe:

- **Mis-alignment**: the difference between what you want and what the other person wants.
- **Mis-understanding**: how your history and previous experiences mean you approach the situation, whilst not knowing what the other person's history and experiences are.

- **Mis-communication**: not clearly stating your meaning and not truly listening to alternative points of view.
- **Mis-trust**: not being clear on how matters might be resolved or not assigning responsibilities for taking action following the conversation.

When a key conversation goes badly, it's because one or more of these are happening. The great news is that there are ways in which all of these can be addressed to make your interactions more successful!

To start with, as you build your skills, these methods will work best where you plan for the key conversation (as best you can without knowing for certain the other person's responses). With practice, however, the methods will become more familiar and natural so that you'll find yourself seeing the 'mis-sing' safety signs. As you gain experience, you'll find you can address the issues more spontaneously in your interactions.

Read each element of what may be 'mis-sing' below and answer the questions where applicable.

Mis-alignment

Whether a conversation you need to have is positive or a difficult message, its successful outcome will still depend on alignment between the wants/needs of all parties to the discussion.

As you prepare for and conduct a conversation to avoid misalignment, remember the following:

- **Resist the urge to 'win'**: keep returning to what you want for you and them from this conversation. Who will you ask for feedback and why?
- **Avoid just staying 'safe'**: remember your goals and don't just cave in to keep the peace.
- **Be open to alternatives**: listen to ideas other than your own about how your goal might be reached—you don't have to have all the answers and it helps enormously if you build them together.
- **Keep asking questions**: by challenging your own mind you will focus it, rather than letting emotion and your physiology take over. By asking them questions you will build a shared understanding.

So how do you achieve that?

It begins with you being absolutely clear about what you want and your motivations for having the conversation. Ask:

- What is it that I *truly* want to get out of this?
- How do I want my relationship with this person to be?
- What is it that I want as an outcome for them?
- How would I behave in this conversation if this was what I truly wanted?

Write down your answers for each key conversation this applies to for you.

Mis-understanding

Our tendency to misunderstand one another when we're entering into a key conversation—even if the conversation is a positive one and begins well—can be about what baggage we bring to the table.

We are all products of our own history—our beliefs, experiences, successes, failures—we have a lot of 'past' through which we view the world, ourselves and others; this can get in our way when we engage in a key conversation, often subconsciously.

Then there is the other person; they bring all of their history with them too, which shapes their responses.

We need to acknowledge this in the tackling of misunderstanding.

Of course, we cannot know everyone else's back-story and, indeed, we don't bring all of our own to every situation. However, when planning for a key conversation we need to be aware of what parts of our history will 'trigger' certain behaviours and responses as well as acknowledging that the same will be true for the other parties in the discussion.

When the conversation is planned (as it is here), then below are some questions for you to consider. Remember to record your answers for the conversations you plan to have.

- What might happen to my behaviour during this conversation?
- Am I normally more prone to 'silence' or 'violence' as a reaction?
- How will I notice when that happens? What will I do?
- What are the emotions that might cause this behaviour?
- How will I identify and label them?
- What can I do to control them?
- What is my history/the story I have created that is generating these emotions?

- Where do they come from? What else has happened to me in my past that may make me feel unsafe in this conversation in the present?
- What facts and evidence do I have that support the story I am telling myself about this conversation? Therefore, is the story true or invented?

As you become more accustomed to asking these questions, you'll be able to use them dynamically in unplanned conversations too.

Mis-communication

When we build ourselves up to having a key conversation by telling ourselves stories about how it's going to go (based on our, sometimes inaccurate, perception through the lens of our history), we can frequently miscommunicate. This is especially so when we don't create safety for the other person so that they can share or process their stories too.

The way to address this is to undertake the following process:

- **Facts:** state some facts. Real facts! If you begin with anything that is incontrovertible, it will get the conversation off to the best start.
- **Conclusions:** say what conclusions those facts *may* have pointed you towards as a way to open up the discussion.
- **Questions:** ask others for *their* facts. What are their conclusions and what is the story behind them? Seek to explore these and be prepared to listen.

- **Possibilities**: express your ideas/thoughts as possibilities, not absolutes. Keep the dialogue positive by being open to new ideas and information.
- **Invitations**: welcome different views and even challenge your own opinion to invite discussion and mean it when you do!
- **Searches**: look for common ground, however small if it's a difficult conversation, and state clearly your agreement. Then build upon that.
- **Differences**: acknowledge openly where differences remain. Try to resolve them by keep asking questions, exploring each other's reasons and looking for possibilities for increasing your common ground.

Mis-trust

If the motivation behind a key conversation comes from what you really want out of it for you and others (Alignment), you enter the conversation having been clear about the causes of your emotions (Understanding) and then conduct the conversation based on facts and genuine exploration to build common ground (Communication), then you've made a great start.

The final part of planning for your key conversation is about avoiding Mistrust, which can occur after the discussion when ownership for seeing outputs through is not clear or action isn't taken. If these behaviours have happened previously, be aware that you may be starting the conversation from a place of mistrust too.

In essence, building trust when it comes to key conversations is about summarising the outcomes and then agreeing for each action the:

- Who.
- What.
- When.
- Follow up.

Now, if your key conversation happens in a work or more formal context, then it may be that your outputs and those responsible will be documented and reviewed, which would be recommended.

When the conversation is of a more personal or informal nature, sending a follow-up document and plan would just look a bit weird! I mean, I'm comfortable with my own particular brand of weird, but there is a line folks! That's not to say, however, that you can't verbally agree the points above and you can always follow up with friendly reminders or updates about completed actions by text or some other informal means.

Seeing things through—doing what you say you're going to do—builds trust in both you and others. If someone else doesn't complete the tasks they committed to, then you'll need to speak to them. That's the time for another key conversation.

Just consider every key conversation as practice. The more you do, the quicker you'll become an expert.

SELF Step 9: Summary

In the 'Compassion' Step you have:

- Learnt that showing compassion to you and others is crucial to the life you want and person you aim to be.
- Understood that effective communication shouldn't just be left to chance when it comes to your intended life.
- Determined which key conversations you need to have with your current network.
- Identified key conversations that you need to have with or to fill gaps in your Top Team.
- Planned for what may be 'mis-sing' in key conversations.

"True freedom is understanding that we have choice in who and what we allow to have power over us."
- Meryl Streep -

THE SELF STEPS – STAGE 4

SELF Fulfilment

Fulfilment – When am I?

We all deserve to feel fulfilled. The great Simon Sinek (I'm a huge fan) describes it as, "*a right and not a privilege*". I couldn't agree more. Living the right life is what we should all be able to do. For each one of us that sense of fulfilment comes from something different; even if society would have us believe that the pursuit of money, a big house, fancy car, several holidays a year and the picture perfect family is what fulfilment *should* look like. It doesn't. *You* define it. For you, it might just be something very different to that poster image of 'success'. It might also be something very different from what you have today.

Whatever you have articulated during the previous 9 SELF Steps as to what you want your life to look like, none of it will happen unless you take action. None of that greater purpose will come to life unless you are compelled by it. The fear of staying as you are and not getting that eulogy you want has to be bigger than the fear of taking the first steps towards something else.

The Fulfilment stage is all about bringing together the pieces of the picture you have been building. The practical and emotional picture; that image of the life you want that drives you forward towards taking action to make it a reality.

These final three Steps are where you make Choices (Step 10) about what you're going to do and really nail down your actions by being specific and targeted. Then it's time to look at creating a success environment, one where you stand the best possible chance of delivering on those intentions and measuring your progress (Growth). Then, finally, you will set out how and when you're going to review your progress and Celebrate (Step 12) how far you've come.

It's time to get specific.

"I don't have regrets.
I make choices and I live with the consequences."
- Unknown -

SELF Step 10

CHOICE

Choice

What is the story behind this Step?

I love the previous quote. It sums me up. I gave up having regrets a long time ago because I realised that it is a totally wasted, destructive emotion. What do regrets do other than hold you in a place in your past that you can do nothing about? Instead, we need to focus you on what you're going to going forward.

Identify choices.

Make decisions.

Take action.

This Step is here because nothing will change unless you start doing something different. I get that this is scary, but that's why together we have done the work to this point to build the picture of the change you want to see and develop the emotional connection with why it is important.

For me, when I had choices to make, some of them meant I had to face into some harsh home truths. I was fortunate enough to have someone who told me the simple truth in a couple of areas of my life and I will be forever grateful to them for that. Someone who had the courage to tell me that the 'family home' I was buying—a definite symbol of my perceived 'success'—was pointless when I didn't have, couldn't have and would never have my own family. That might sound cruel. It really wasn't. It was delivered with a straight-forward honesty that I couldn't argue with and nor could I be offended by. I needed to be told and here was someone with no 'skin in the game' as far as my circumstances were concerned, which meant they were able to deliver that truth without it hurting. It was factual. It was actually an act of immense kindness because it stopped me from tethering myself to a life I no longer wanted based on an illusion of something I would never have.

The other thing about Choice is that you have to examine all your options. Frequently, when you feel like the world is spinning so fast your head hurts, it's hard to see that you have any choices at all. I'm here to tell you, based on my life and work experience, you often have way more choice and more control than you perceive. That choice is true for situations, people, your emotions and behaviours. You get to choose them. That was my personal breakthrough: no one gets to choose how I feel other than me. It's a hard one sometimes. A person says and does something that provokes a reaction in you. Yet, I learnt it was about allowing that initial reaction or emotion to pass. To observe it, but not rely on it. Emotions, as they say, are not facts. Indeed, has the emotion you're feeling got anything to do with the current situation or is it actually a hangover from something in your past? It's better to examine that emotional reaction and see whether it was fitting to the situation or serving you positively. Then make a choice about how to *respond*. There is a clear distinction between a reaction and a response. Now don't get me wrong, I don't deal with my life like some emotionless Vulcan who only sees the world through logic. Far from it! I do, however, try to be more measured these days and far less reliant on the first emotion that floods through me.

A number of the choices I had to make in the period after I had to rebuild my life were tough ones. However, it was developing a plan that helped me pull myself out of the quagmire bit by bit. That's not to say all of the plan or the choices were right, but at least I made some, made progress and moved forward at a time when it would have been so easy to stay stuck.

For me, there were short-term, immediate choices like saying "*yes*" to more opportunities and living more in the moment when it came to meeting new people or chance encounters. I certainly became more open, friendly, and communicative with strangers. I chose to pay strangers a compliment rather than merely thinking it inside my own head. That sounds like something small, but it honestly has so much feel-good factor attached. I highly recommend it! I was also fortunate enough to be able to 'gift' myself a 10-week stay in a beautiful rental property. It was a step towards living alone for the first time in three years whilst I was waiting to get myself a more permanent home. That was one of the best things I did. In my still-fragile state of dipping my toe into the waters of a new life, to have somewhere safe in a close-knit community was perfect. I know it was a luxury not everyone could afford, but my point is that it's about the small kindnesses to yourself, whatever your circumstances and your budget. I would not previously have taken such a decision, but I chose to put my needs first and not have to be 100% 'strong' or 'ready' for my new life immediately.

Then came the bigger choices. These were decisions about my permanent home. The life I wanted. My future. I'll admit that these took a bit more working through, but it also taught me that the right thing will show itself. Honestly, it always does. I know that might sound a bit 'woo' for some and I'm not a great one for always advocating the power of the 'universe' or believing entirely in 'manifestation' (I've not yet manifested that situation where it rains shoes) but I do think that what's right will reveal itself. Sometimes you just need to be patient and that's a virtue that many of us in the immediacy of our current world just don't possess! I also don't believe, though, that I am uniquely blessed; that things just fell into place in my life, because my life previously had, through the choices I'd made, frequently fallen apart. Yet, I know that when it came to choices around the big things, the path that I should take invariably came into view. I just had to wait and be open to seeing it because it wasn't always in the form I imagined.

Here's the thing that you need to remember about choices . . . they are rarely irreversible. Even if reversing them might be a pain in the arse, they can usually be reversed. So just make a decision and go with it. "*Choose*" was the best advice that my coach gave me. It's so simple, but effective.

When I find myself procrastinating, faffing about, stuck or not moving forwards, I now just say, "*Oh for goodness sake, just choose!*" and it instantly shifts the barriers. Try it. Whether you're standing in the supermarket trying to decide whether to buy apple or orange juice, or if it's between this house location or that—just choose. Doing that has helped to prevent many a sleepless night!

Why is this Step important?
Have you ever procrastinated? Been indecisive? Not taken action because you couldn't determine which way to leap? Felt stuck?

We've all done it!

From these shoes or those shoes, to this job or that job, to this partner or that one (OK, so maybe I haven't always had that many choices with the last one!) we've all struggled to make choices at one time or another.

When I felt completely stuck by the vast sea of choice and opportunity that lay before me—but found that landscape totally terrifying—I know there were times when I was paralysed into inaction. I knew I'd made a wealth of mistakes getting to that point and was desperate to avoid another.

That's why this Step is important. It's about acknowledging that you don't have to do everything at once. You just need to set a few clear intentions—how many is up to you (you get to choose that too!) —so that you get going. As my idol, Matthew Hussey, would say, "*Just get the car moving*". It's such wise advice. Just do something. Anything. Just make a plan that you commit to. Yes, you might need to adjust that plan along the way but accept that as part of the process. Exactly like driving a car, you have to tweak the wheel this way and that all the time to stay on course. In the first instance, this is just about getting some things in place that make you feel like you're building the life that will create your eulogy.

You're here because you *want* something to be different. You *need* it to be different. Don't get to this point and then give up. I love the saying, *"You didn't come this far to only come this far"*. Ain't that the truth!

If you struggle to find the motivation to make change for you, do it for someone else. Be their role model. I try to be a better me for my niece and nephew. I want them to see how you can overcome challenges, be courageous and grab the world. I want to inspire them to go further than I ever will. It's worth a bit of my own pain and discomfort if I can be that to them. Find the person or people—either within your life or as an external group—that you want to inspire through your action. Go do it for them.

Choice is important because it leads to action. Only action will bring about change. All the words, thoughts and good intentions won't make the shift you need to. Choice is where courage meets action and ignites something new to happen.

Before proceeding to the activities associated with this Step, re-familiarise yourself with the following outputs you have achieved so far:

- Your problem statement.
- The prioritised causes from your Fishbone exercise.

- The outputs from your people network Impact Assessment.

These will assist you with identifying the issues you need to tackle.

Practical Activities

ACTIVITY 10.1

Consolidating your actions

From all the activities, thinking and actions you've gathered so far, it's time to get to the sharp end of pulling together your finalised plan. When making change it's important to keep your confidence high and, as we discovered earlier, the key to confidence is competence.

So, starting to take action—just a few small, initial steps—and doing so quickly, will really help you to feel competent that you *can* make change. Get the car moving, remember.

Refer to the headline B.E.I.N.G. action plan you've developed so far. Look first at the actions you already have and consider for each one:

- Is this action still relevant now that I have gained more insights? (If not, then delete it or move it to the bottom of your list to come back to later).
- Is there anything about this action that I need to amend before I build more detail around it?

Remember:

- Keep the things that will serve you in achieving your 'ideal' life vision and eulogy.

- Keep those that will address the root causes of your problem statement.
- Keep those that will ensure you live by your Character Commitment.

Discard any that don't help you to do these things.

In deciding which actions to add, keep or delete, you might want to ask the following questions:

- If there were no barriers at all (e.g. finances, skills, time, emotions), what action would you take?
- For what would you like to be remembered? What legacy do you want to leave?
- What's working in your life right now that you could aim to do more of?
- What else is possible for you to change?

Next, add in any *new* actions that you believe need to be carried out as a result of the insights you've gained; this is so that you have a complete list of all the things you think you need to do. It may be, for example, that one action you identified earlier now needs breaking down into smaller actions to make it more achievable.

Adding a new action at this stage involves stating the headline action in the 'B' (Behaviour) part of your B.E.I.N.G. action plan. You might already know some of the specific details for the 'E' (Explanation) box. If you do, fill those in now, but we will return to completing those in the next activity.

Get all your actions down—at least the Behaviour section— before moving onto the next activity.

PRACTICAL ACTIVITIES

ACTIVITY 10.2

Getting specific

Now that you have all your actions listed out, it's time to finalise getting specific about what each one entails. Completing the 'E' (Explanation) section of your action plan in full. These details are a vital part of setting yourself up for success.

This is because, by breaking down each action and detailing out exactly what you need to do, it has the following benefits:

- The objective feels less overwhelming because you can see the smaller activities that you need to do to achieve it.
- Completing each individual activity will give you a sense of achievement and progress, which helps keep you motivated.
- You will be building belief in your competence to make change by completing elements of each action, which will increase your confidence.

Set out the steps you'll need to take to complete each action on your plan. Be as detailed as you can so that the path from where you are to the action being completed is clear.

Practical Activities

ACTIVITY 10.3

Setting completion goals

Now that you have a list of the main actions you need to achieve and have detailed out the interim steps to get you there, this means that the Behaviour and Explanation sections of your action plan are complete.

The next exercise is to put your actions into the sequence order of the time in which they need to be started and completed.

You can have more than one action 'in play' to be completed at any time depending on the nature of the action. Remember, however, not to overwhelm yourself by trying to do too much at once. Change can be hard, so ensure your success by being realistic about what you can get done.

To complete this, fill in the 'G' (Goal) section of your plan. A date needs to be put in for both when the action needs to *start* and then by when it needs to be *completed*.

NOTE: the order in which actions are completed might be different to the order in which they start, depending on the content of the action.

PRACTICAL ACTIVITIES

ACTIVITY 10.4
Who can help you?

You've done a lot of work thinking about the conversations that you'll need to have with those around you as you make the transition from the life you have to the life you want.

It helps always to have allies in life, that's why the 'N' of the B.E.I.N.G. action planning model standards for 'Network'. Who do you have who can help you complete an action? Who could you speak to about it? Who will be a supporter?

You might want to look again at your 'Top Team' because they should be your first go-to people, but it is very possible that the person that can help you achieve an action is someone outside this group. This person may be a subject matter expert, your boss, or someone else you know you can rely on, but who you wouldn't necessarily call in the early hours when you're in a bit of a fix!

Fill in the 'Network' section of your action plan as the last activity in the Choice Step.

SELF Step 10: Summary

You'll have filled in a lot of your plan by this point and you'll see that the final column of the B.E.I.N.G. structure ('Impact') remains incomplete.

We'll be returning to look at performance, measurement and rewards in Step II, 'Growth'.

In the 'Choice' Step you have:

- Learnt that there are always choices, even when it can seem as though there are none!
- Understood that making choices is key to taking action, and only by taking action will change happen.
- Reviewed all the choices you have.
- Established all your actions and detailed out the Steps to complete them.
- Set goals for the start and end of each objective.
- Identified who can support you with achieving your objectives.

"The way you craft the legacy of your rejection can result in some of the most meaningful wins of your life."
- Matthew Hussey -

SELF Step 11

Growth

What is the story behind this Step?

I don't know about you, but I used to have a very negative relationship with failure. It's why the F in my S.E.L.F.I.S.H. model stands for exactly that. I can tell you though, that the 'F' could've stood for something else entirely, huh?!

Anyway, back to the point . . .

We need to change our mindset about failure to be able to be kinder to ourselves. Accepting that you'll get things wrong is all part of Growth. It's been a challenge for me to get comfortable with this (and, of course, when I fail it does still sting!) but I see it now as progress, opportunity and learning.

You'll learn how to shift your thinking about failure in the activities at the end of this section.

Suffice it to say, though, that during my life transformation I got things wrong. I trusted people who didn't deserve it and who, at times, actively worked to dismantle me. Have I let that stop me trusting anyone? No. I don't want to be *that*

177

woman. I can understand that some people openly say that they trust no-one, but that's not a life I'd choose. We weren't designed to make it through this life alone. Not everyone is untrustworthy. As I've mentioned before—and I'll say it again because I think it is so vital to our sense of fulfilment—deep personal connections enrich our lives and help us to live longer. I don't understand why anyone wouldn't want to have that. Do those connections potentially make us vulnerable? Of course, but as with anything, it's how we get back up that matters, not how we fall down; our response is for what we will be measured and judged.

The most important lesson I learnt about failure was how to prevent it. It was understanding that those that succeed had learnt—through their own failures—where and how their failures could happen. More importantly, they had mastered the art of putting measures in place to create an environment conducive to success. One where failure was minimised. Not eliminated, but minimised. Managed. Taken account of. Anticipated. Counteracted.

This is where knowing about you comes in. It's where all the work you have done so far to uncover who you are, what you want and how you want your life to be, converge. You need to know what causes *you* to fail. What are your weak points? Under what circumstances do these occur?

I'll tell you where it doesn't happen. Willpower. That will never be the reason you fail. It will frequently be the excuse that you or others use. Like I said earlier, that's nonsense. Willpower doesn't exist.

However, when I've talked to people about change during

my career—and away from work—I find they have a good idea about what they want to change, even if they're not sure why that is or what sits at the root cause. When the conversation then turns to the reasons why they're not already making that change ... this is the point when things usually get a little uncomfortable.

Whether the thing they want to change is something at work, at home or perhaps about their lifestyle, typically somewhere in amongst the reasons why they've not started or succeeded at change is the word 'willpower'.

"I don't have it."

"I don't have enough of it."

"I can't stick at anything!"

Wow, anything, really? You sure?

Their words are often accompanied by comparisons to people they deem to have the willpower they lack.

Well, let's firmly stick a pin in the 'willpower' balloon. Willpower isn't something that some people are blessed with whilst others are not.

Lacking willpower is not why you're still paying your monthly gym membership even though you haven't been back since your induction session. Having it isn't the reason the friend you signed up with has been doing five HIIT classes per week and has never looked better.

You innate 'lack of willpower' isn't why you start a new healthy eating regime every Monday and then on Wednesday night you eat the entire 'family' bag of tortilla chips whilst watching the latest must-see TV series. Conversely, it doesn't contribute to why your partner completes 20 minutes of yoga every day without fail.

Willpower is not in our DNA. It's not like eye colour. It doesn't determine whether or not your hair is curly. It's not genetically gifted to us . . . or not.

Those successful people that you're comparing yourself with? They don't have any more willpower than you have.

Whaaaaaaatttttt??!

I know, no more excuses, right?

Sorry about that. Actually, that's not true. I'm not sorry at all. Ridding the world of the excuse of 'not having sufficient willpower' has sort of become my thing.

Now you want to know what is the difference between those that succeed and those that don't?

OK, so there might be differences in physicality, opportunity and resources, that's for sure. I don't argue with that. But if you put you and someone else in similar situations, and one of you succeeds and one of you fails, it won't be about differences in willpower.

What it *is* about, is the environment you each create. By putting in place the right circumstances for success, you can achieve that success. I know, I didn't know this for many years either. I thought it was down to sheer grit and determination as to whether I got through something or achieved the result I wanted.

That all changed when I started to look at what made people successful and, more particularly, what made them successful at *change*.

In my case, I knew that significant things needed to change if I wasn't going to keep repeating the same patterns that I'd perpetuated over decades. It wasn't only the patterns that needed to change, though, it was how well I held fast to new behaviours. How did I turn old habits into new habits? How could I prevent myself from falling off the proverbial wagon? How did I not give up and slip back to old ways?

I knew I was going to need ... something ... to hold me true to the course I wanted to be on. I knew that I didn't want to look back at the next decades of my life from some unwanted vantage point where I found myself, one again, having veered off and got lost.

One thing I did know from my time in HR was that it wasn't enough to have a system of rewards. Whilst those are important, they alone will not suffice.

"*What does work then?*", I hear you cry!

Well, lucky enough for you, Dear Reader, I learnt over time what those 'secrets' are. In fact, they are not secrets at all. They are simply the things that need to replace our reliance on willpower if we really want to change.

Good news is, there are only six of them and they are, for the most part, easy to implement.

I call these elements of change 'CHARGE' (you'll have noticed way before now that I do love a good acronym!) because it's all about making sure you put your own personal battery at as near to 100% power to ensure you are successful. These elements are:

- Costs
- Habits
- Abilities
- Relationships
- Gratification
- Environment

In the activities at the end of this Step you'll get to learn more about each element and what you need to do to put them in place for your particular transformation.

Why is this Step important?
We don't grow if we do nothing.

We don't grow if we don't act.

We don't grow if we stick with old (usually, bad) habits. We don't grow by accident.

We don't grow if we're not motivated to be different.

We don't grow unless we fail and learn.

In my previous pursuit of perfection in my life, I sort of knew this, but my efforts were around being flawless as a way of achieving success. That wasn't realistic and it wasn't success. Yes, I achieved things, but the negative consequences and the personal costs were so high that it became detrimental in my life.

If you want to grow you need to become more considered and purposeful about it. There needs to be structure to the choices you make and there must be a way that you measure progress—the mere fact of doing that will spur you on. By putting in place the right circumstances for you to succeed and having people who will walk, run and cheer alongside you, are all essential. Accepting that you are unlikely to make it on your own is a key part of this Step. In fact, its fundamental to the entire SELF Steps concept—who you have around you is essential for a fulfilled life.

Putting you in the best place possible for *Being* yourSELF is what this book is all about. Who wants to have a mediocre life? Who doesn't want to leave a legacy? Who doesn't want their time here to matter to someone? Who wants to think that 20 years after they died that no-one would remember them?

If the thought of any of those being true for you horrifies you, then you need to act. To adapt, learn and grow throughout your life. No cavalry is arriving to make it happen for you. Those who 'make it' do so through concerted effort—even when we like to think they were 'lucky' or just 'gifted'. In my experience, gifts and luck take an enormous amount of hard work! You're either prepared to do what it takes or not. The choice whether to grow is yours.

"The bad days are more important than the good days.
If you write or exercise or meditate or cook
when you don't feel like it,
then you maintain the habit.
And if you maintain the habit,
all you need is time."
- James Clear -

Practical Activities

ACTIVITY 11.1

How can you make sure you're having an impact?

When we measure our progress towards an objective it helps us to:

- Know what 'success' looks like and when we will have reached it.
- Stay motivated towards our intention.
- Feel like the end result is achievable.
- Create some challenge with ourselves, which makes it fun!
- Take corrective action quickly if we're going off course.

For these reasons, understanding the impact we want our actions to have is vital.

Now that you have all your actions identified and know who you need to speak to about your plan, it's time to undertake the last step of completing your action plan, which is to put some impact measurements in place for each objective.

To do this, ask:

- What will be the outcome of having taken this action?
- How will I *ultimately* know that the action I have taken has been successful?

- What will I see as being different from before I took action?
- What will others observe as having changed?
- Whilst I am working towards the outcome, what metrics can I put in place to show whether I am on or off track?
- What interim milestones can I set? (We call this 'fast feedback' because it helps you to quickly course-correct so that you don't go too far off plan).

These measures shouldn't be solely about 'completing' an action. They need to be tangible outcomes and results that show that change is being made; that things in your life will be different because of the activity you've done.

Complete your action plan by filling in the 'I' (Impact) section for each of the items in your action plan.

PRACTICAL ACTIVITIES

ACTIVITY 11.2

How to CHARGE up your change battery

In case you are concerned that there is another whirlwind of activity coming over the horizon, you can breathe easy. The great news is that throughout this programme you've already been charging up your change battery—perhaps without knowing it. Within the Steps you've done there have been several activities and preparatory mindsets that are already designed to help you to start and stick at change, which will lead to your success.

What is left to do is work at putting in place the final pieces that will make sure you're not relying on willpower any longer.

Below is a more detailed reminder of the six elements of my CHARGE model. These include the questions you need to ask yourself to make use of each element towards your success.

- **Costs:** understand what the costs are of NOT making the change. How will it pain you? Use that as leverage to motivate you. Also put in place milestones to achieve and incentives as reward as for each one you reach.
- **Habits:** set a clear standard for who and what you want to be so that you know what you're aiming for. How

do you want your life to look going forwards? Who do you know and look up to that already has these habits? Keep this standard close at hand to refer to whenever you have a 'wobble' (which it's normal to have, by the way).

- **Abilities**: understand what capabilities you already have that you can use to help achieve your goal. Be clear about where the gaps are and what skills you might have to learn. Plan for any moments of failure (see the next activity) and be explicit about how you will overcome them so you can implement that tactic immediately.

- **Relationships**: who do you have around you already who could help you to achieve your goals? Who might be a distraction and detractor? Decide in advance how you might deal with them by thinking through how you will explain what you're trying to achieve and why.

- **Gratification**: how will making this change positively impact your life? Will it impact the lives of others? Who can you be a role model for? Keeping a promise to someone else is a greater motivator than keeping one to ourselves, so set clearly in your mind who you want to make proud.

- **Environment**: how can you build the new behaviours into existing things you do? Doing this makes it easier to adopt new behaviours and stick to them. Where and how can you place reminders around you of your intentions and actions so that they stay at the forefront of your mind?

You'll see how much of this you have begun to build on already. Great, huh?!

Take some time now to put the last few elements in place that will make your changes stick.

PRACTICAL ACTIVITIES

ACTIVITY 11.3

How to handle failure and setbacks

So far, we've focused on what it's going to take to get started with and achieve your change plan. Yet we all know that, in life, there are good times and bad. Despite our best laid plans, sometimes we will still get blown off course.

We all fail—multiple times in our lives—never more so than when we're trying something different or where we're inexperienced. It's important that we embrace the opportunity that 'failure' provides for us to learn—about ourselves, others or new skills—and use that to propel us forward rather than staying stuck beating ourselves up for getting it 'wrong'.

Think about a recent failure or failures you've had. Break down those experiences in the following way in order to reframe them into a positive experience:

- **Analyse**: where and how did it *specifically* occur, rather than seeing it all as one total 'failure'?
- **Acquire**: what did this failure teach you?
- **Accept**: how can you make peace with yourself about what happened?
- **Adapt**: what can you take forwards to do differently to prevent it from happening again?

One of the best ways to be prepared for change is to consider what will put your achievement at risk. Thinking about and planning for failure isn't about being defeatist before you've even started—it's smart thinking. Knowing where and when your weak points may occur means you can put in place strategies to spot when that happens and counter-act it in advance.

So how do we do that? What can you do to stay focused on your change activity, particularly on those days when you're just not feeling it?

You can do that by completing the following questions. Think about them both in terms of your individual actions and the overall plan.

- **When are you likely to fail?** Be critical of your plan and get really specific (and honest) about potential failure points. Highlight where you think they'll arise.
- **What can you do to prevent each one?** Again, be very targeted about this. What actions and practices can you put in place to pull the situation round when failure beckons?
- **What will be your mindset when you fail?** You get to choose your attitude to failure, so what will it be? Is there a phrase you can repeat? A motivational quote you can refer to so that your mindset remains positive?
- **Who in your network can help you?** Which members of your network can support you with which types of

failure? What help will you need to ask them for? Can you get their assistance in advance?

Set your failure plan in place now, taking account of all the potential failure points you've identified in your action plan.

SELF Step 11: Summary

In the 'Growth' Step you have:

- Learnt that failure is part of life and an opportunity to improve and grow.
- Cemented the idea that being successful at change isn't about willpower!
- Understood the Impact of your actions and how you'll measure it.
- Discovered how to CHARGE up your change battery.
- Challenged your mindset about failure.
- Made a plan for when you fail.

"The more you praise and celebrate your life,
The more there is in life to celebrate."
- Oprah Winfrey -

SELF Step 12

CELEBRATE

Celebrate

What is the story behind this Step?

It took me such a long time in my life to celebrate myself. It's not what I was raised to do. I don't think that makes me unusual and I certainly didn't have a tough upbringing or an unhappy home life—quite the opposite. It's just that, in our very British way, we didn't 'shout' about ourselves. Moving quietly through life was kind of my family's thing, despite how rowdy we could be amongst ourselves! It took over four decades and, in more recent times, some immense patience from my coach, friend and business associate, Cliff Sewell, for me to accept that I wanted to share my inner light with others. That celebrating who and what I was as a person was fundamental to what I wanted to do in life. That what I really wanted was to create spaces—both physically and emotionally—within others to enable them to have the courage of being themselves. I have to say, that these 'others' that I've worked with have often—but not exclusively—been women.

Now, let me qualify that. My work has never been about doing anything at the expense of men. I love men. Sometimes I have loved them a bit too much (refer to 'All The Twats I Met Along The Way'). I do firmly believe that men currently get a bit of a rough ride. I have sympathy with why they probably feel that they can't do or say anything right. Don't get me wrong, there are those that don't say or do a lot that's right. Yet, we have to accept that we are *all* products of the time, culture and environment that we grow up and live within (for men in the UK this has been a white, heterosexual, male-dominated environment for a *very* long time). Now it's time for that to change. To be fair, it has been changing—very gradually and through the cumulative efforts of many both privately and publicly—for a while. Yet, as we've learnt throughout this book, change can be slow and arduous even just for us as individuals— we'll fail, fall over and sometimes want to pull the duvet up over our heads to avoid it. Now imagine that we're trying to make that change collectively as a society and not just with respect to those who are—possibly accurately, but maybe rather cruelly—labelled 'male, pale and stale'.

This is not about 'shouting' those men down. Far from it. All that does is silence them. It doesn't change their mindset. Silence is all that shouting—whether actually or on social media—does about any such issue where one group feels disadvantaged in some way versus another. Shouting at the perceived offenders may temper their behaviour publicly, but they will still think the same way privately. Amongst themselves they will likely still speak the same way. Sometimes they will still behave the same way, certainly covertly and, for some, overtly.

Let's look at it a different way. Unless we create safe spaces for those whom we want to change to voice their thoughts, feelings and raise questions in an effort to understand what and how they need to be different, then we'll change nothing because there will be no education.

Like I said, this isn't about getting at men, it's just that I have been a woman all my life and that's why I know we need to help women especially to get more comfortable with celebrating themselves. The men—not all of them, I accept— are doing much better at it than we are, so I'm going to let them keep doing what they're doing whilst us ladies up our game on our own terms.

I know that celebrating ourselves can feel quite uncomfortable. I am sure I am not the only one who was raised to consider it a little 'unseemly'. I'm sure it's why I still find selfies and social media a bit cringe. Oh, how the subsequent generations are different! Yet, we know that this in itself has created its own set of problems.

Women also don't help themselves. Women are not as good as they ought to be at celebrating other women. I think it comes back to a time when women were pitted against each other to secure the best 'mate'—in many ways those days still feel like today, don't they?

Somehow, we're encouraged to see other women as sources of competition, not collaboration. Whilst, at the same time, we can be criticised for not conforming to the idea of some universal 'sisterhood' that we must all sign up to be part of—regardless of whether we like what other sisters might be doing in that hood. It's no wonder we're confused!

Like most women, I have examples of where members of the sisterhood have taken umbrage at me. I used to let it worry me, but now I don't. That comes back to knowing who I am and what my standards are. If someone isn't like-valued or part of my tribe, which I don't see as needing to be ALL women, then that is OK.

One of those examples occurred when I was trying to rebuild my transformed life and was giving various things a go. I decided that I would try yoga. I felt like it was also a good way to make new friends and strengthen my network. There was a beginner's class that, as fortune would have it, was running just over the road from where I was living at the time. I expected that it would be predominantly attended by women (it was all women) and thought it was a good way to meet like-minded people whilst learning a new skill. Perfect.

I did enjoy it, despite the fact my bubble was conclusively burst in the very first session. As you would expect we (eight women) were each asked to introduce ourselves to the rest of the group and say why we were taking the beginners course. When it came to my turn, I said exactly what I wrote above, that I was there to learn a new skill that I was interested in and, at the same time, thought it would be great to meet other people who were interested in the same activity. All good. Or so I thought.

When the class was over and we were leaving, one of the other ladies turned to me and said, "*Looking like you, no-one will want to be your friend*". It took me a moment to take in what she'd said and process what she meant. Why would how I look mean I wouldn't make friends? My mind instantly went to where most female minds would go: am I *that* ugly?

What is *wrong* with me? Now, I don't have tickets on myself and my appearance—let me just make that clear. What I mean by that is that I think I look 'OK'. I was, by then, several months into my first ever serious fitness regime and making a much more concerted effort to look after myself. I don't really have many complaints about my body and this was definitely because I had consciously chosen to do something about how I felt about myself—both mind and body. What I realised this lady meant was that my physical appearance was a threat in some way. The way *I* looked made *her* feel insecure about herself. She wouldn't want to be seen with me, regardless of who I was as a person. Yet, apart from that brief introduction to each other at the start of the class, we'd not had the chance to chat/get to know each other because we were all too busy trying to not fart—let's be honest, from the front as well as the back—whilst doing the 'downward dog'. However, she'd taken one look at me and decided I was to be avoided. Now, that's her choice. We all make our first assessments about a person by the way they look—we like to say we don't because that's the 'correct' way to be, but reality is that for hundreds of thousands of years our visual assessment of what could be the 'enemy' was our first line of defence in terms of our own survival. So, we have to accept in the present day that this is how are brains are still wired. Our laws and society have evolved, of course, but our basic, primitive brains biologically have not. It's why we cross the street to avoid someone we have never met but 'don't like the look of'. It's what we do. It's how we are.

My point is, not everyone will like you. Not everyone will celebrate you. We know this. We just have to *really* know that in order to have a life that isn't encumbered by the judgements and negativity of others. It's our life. Our standards. Our terms. Let those others do their thing. You do yours. Try not to criticise them, even if they criticise you. If we all chose to live a bit more like this, I honestly think the world would be a better place and we'd all be happier—and a heck of a lot nicer to each other!

That's why the last of the SELF Steps is about celebration—yours and others'.

Let's do this together.

Why is this Step important?
If you don't celebrate you, who will? Yes, there will be people who will be happy for your achievements and those friends or family members that will be there for the big moments of your life. You may have already established those when you've put key people in your life into the 12 character types earlier.

Here, though, I'm talking about the little wins. The micro-moments of positivity that others might not see or even know about. The things in your head that you need to acknowledge as small successes. That deep breath you take rather than sighing when a work colleague annoys you. It's looking for the positive in something your child has done that is a patience-testing disaster in every other respect!

It's the small wins as much as, even more than, the big ones that I want to encourage you to focus on here. That's because it's those small wins that will spur you on. The many tiny changes that will make up the bigger change—they are what add together to make progress.

It is also vitally important that you factor in times for reviewing *how* you're doing, both where things are going well and where you might not be making the gains you intended. Fronting into where you are off-plan and taking action swiftly will also keep you motivated—you should also celebrate the fact that you have quickly arrested any negative situations!

The point of the SELF Steps is that it isn't a finite programme. The idea is that you make choices, you make progress, you review where you are—against your Character Commitment, your ideal eulogy and with your B.E.I.N.G. action plan—and then you adjust, plan the next actions and move forwards. It's not a 'big bang' approach, but a carefully thought-through sequence of iterative Steps. Did you spot what I did there?

That's why the Celebrate Step is critical. To encourage you to enjoy the journey as well as the destination.

"The last mile is always the least crowded."
- James Clear -

Practical Activities

Activity 12.1

Celebrating successes

Just as important as the plan for setbacks, is knowing when and how you will celebrate your successes.

I talked previously about rewards and how they can be part of a system of motivators, but celebrating your successes is about hitting the key milestones of your change . . . and knowing what those are.

This isn't about being arrogant—the gesture doesn't have to be grand—but it is about taking a moment to say 'well done' to yourself for having the courage and commitment to make changes and go after the life you want. Remember, there will be many who will not be brave enough to do what you are doing and some who may try to derail you with their negativity. That's why a moment to 'high-five' yourself is permitted!

Take some time to think about, identify and plan for:

- Which milestones you plan to celebrate.
- How you will celebrate them.
- Who you will choose to enjoy your successes with (if anyone).

Practical Activities

ACTIVITY 12.2
Collecting feedback

You've got all the parts you need now to move forwards, but it's important that as you do so you also take time out to reflect—not least because we can all be guilty sometimes of not giving ourselves credit for how far we've come. This can be especially true on the days when you're struggling to stay motivated and on-plan as it is when things are going well.

That's why seeking the input and perspective of others (remember to do so from those who you trust and who's opinion you value for sound reasons), can help you to see why you should be celebrating progress.

Think about and write down your answers to the following:

- Who will you ask for feedback and why?
- What feedback will you specifically seek from each of those people about the changes you're making?
- How will you build what's working into your life/ habits to keep it going?

Plan for this now and set reminders for when you're going to seek feedback.

*"Celebrate what you've accomplished,
but raise the bar a little higher each time you succeed."*
- Mia Hamm -

PRACTICAL ACTIVITIES

ACTIVITY 12.3
Conducting a review

The Steps in this programme are designed to be iterative: you build the plan, make the changes, review progress, and adjust the plan. Then repeat that cycle. You can go back and repeat any Step at any time, as well as build a new plan for the next stage of your journey towards the life you want, once you've completed all your initial actions.

Know also, that it's OK to amend the plan at any stage of your transformation. As new information emerges and your vision of the life you want continues to evolve, then it makes sense to tweak your plan accordingly. There is no rule that says you need to stick rigidly to a plan that is no longer serving you!

Instead, be sure to continue using the tools and techniques in the Steps to keep in the front of your mind what's important to you, why you're making the change and how you're going to get to the fulfilled life you want.

That's why I want to encourage you as the final activity to put in place a review process.

Set yourself these tasks:

- At what points/regularity will you conduct a review of your plan? Put these in your diary!
- Who (if anyone) will you speak to about that review?
- Which of the exercise outputs will it be most important for you to be reminded of when you conduct that review?
- How will you update and store the revised version of your action plan?

SELF Step 12: Summary

In the 'Celebrate' Step you have:

- Learnt that celebrating your achievements—if only with yourself—is important recognition of your progress.
- Accepted that not everyone will appreciate your success, but that's OK.
- Established when and how you will celebrate your successes.
- Determined from whom you will seek feedback and perspective on your progress.
- Identified how and when you will conduct a review of your B.E.I.N.G. action plan.

Time for some final pearls of wisdom . . .

We've covered a lot of ground in this book. I've demanded plenty from you, I won't lie. Yet, I hope that when you look back on it, you can see the jigsaw pieces of your future falling into place. Who you are, what you want, who you want to share it with—you can feel that light you've dimmed for so long, reigniting.

I spent a long time thinking and doing the wrong stuff, so my aim has always been to pass on those lessons and to steer you more quickly and successfully towards *Being* yourSELF than I had managed for most of my life.

Yet, I can say—hand on heart—that I am forever grateful for the changes I was thrown into making in my life. Whilst I would have appreciated a 'gentler' nudge than they provided, without them, I wouldn't be where I am today. And where I am today is . . . *Being Unapologetically mySELF*. That's how I would describe it. Every quirk, idiosyncrasy, mannerism, imperfection, ability, weakness, strength—I'll never stop trying to grow and improve—but I accept them all for putting me right where I am right now because it's right where I need to be.

After I went through my transformation, I smashed through my first action plan and now I have one that constantly evolves as I move forwards, living true to who I am. I still revisit the activities in these Steps, review and adjust, then set off again with renewed focus and even more 'fuck it' in my attitude!

Have I made mistakes? Of course. I have loved and lost again. I have stumbled and got back up. I have discovered new things about myself and others and refined my vision for the life I want because of them. Yet, the initial course it set me on has remained steadfast, as has who I (re)discovered I was at my core.

I don't want to write a long goodbye—not least because this isn't one. Well, it *is* a goodbye to Twats, I admit. It's much more than that, though.

It's a 'hello' to a new you.

It's a 'welcome' to the *Being* yourSELF tribe.

Most of all, it's a 'let me take you by the hand and accompany you the rest of the way' because as the saying goes, "*We're all just walking each other home.*" (Ram Dass).

It's time for you to find 'home'.

Other books by Carolyn Hobdey

All The Twats I Met Along The Way
(Second edition, Autumn 2021)

What happens when you so deeply believe something you were told as a child that it becomes the driving force behind almost every thought, feeling and action for the rest of your life, until you decide to take complete control and change your life entirely?

For decades, Carolyn Hobdey believed she was 'trouble' and if she wasn't 'nicer' she'd spend her days alone and unloved.

All The Twats I Met Along The Way is the first in Carolyn's 'Twats Trilogy' and tells the tale of crappy boyfriends, sickening sexual encounters, manipulative men, love triangles, unsupportive and unsupported medical diagnoses ... and that's just in the first few pages! From porn-addicted boyfriends who go from fitties to owners of 'dad bods,' to car crashes and boob jobs. Marriage to a lover who became more like a brother (and who harboured a secret Carolyn could not have foreseen) and later a relationship with a man and his 'ready-made family' that exposes a damaging case of coercive control and narcissism. Carolyn's story exposes the unrelenting pull of the child-parent relationship—even in adulthood—and all the messiness, self-esteem issues and confusion that can cause.

Redefining SELFISH: No Guilt. No Regrets.
(Autumn 2021)

Redefining SELFISH comes at an urgent time when women are reporting worsening levels of anxiety and growing mental health concerns and are increasingly initiating divorce. Calls to domestic violence helplines are on the rise and, of course, the pandemic has had a massive impact.

The S.E.L.F.I.S.H model created by Carolyn Hobdey guides the reader through how to give up feeling guilty about taking some time out, instead placing ourselves at the top of our 'to do' list and acknowledging the benefits to us and those around us of making ourselves 'better'. Its purpose—and that of the whole Redefining SELFISH concept—is to encourage self-kindness, develop confidence and shift mindsets from harmful to helpful.

The Everyday Girls Guide to Living in Truth, Self-Love, and Acceptance
(Autumn 2021)

The Everyday Girls Guide to Living in Truth. Self-Love, and Acceptance is the perfect resource of understanding, compassion, and support for teen girls as they navigate this exciting and sometimes daunting chapter of their life.

Including guidance and wisdom from 19 incredible teen girl mentors from around the world.

This book is brought to you by She Speaks Media, a platform dedicated to creating resources that spark transformation in women and teen girls around the world. Founded by Leanne MacDonald, a Spiritual Psychology Coach, New Thought Practitioner, Published Author, and Mum of Four.

Twats at Work!
(2023)

An extensive and illustrious career took Carolyn all the way to the boardroom in some of the World's largest employers as she became a leader for numerous of our most internationally recognised brands.

Carolyn has worked with many great people. She has also encountered quite a few Twats.

'Twats at Work' provides a peak behind the curtain of corporate life and introduces us to the numerous characters she met; from those that asked for a company policy to address an employee's problem body-odour, through the maverick who could only manage by referring to his 'lead-by-numbers' manual and on to the Executive Board that bore an uncanny resemblance to the British comedy 'W1A'.

This book is for anyone who has ever been led. It is especially for those who have ever been led badly.

Carolyn's experience is that there is an awful lot of the latter, so this book is also for anyone who is a leader and wants to learn how they might do that better.

It examines the great leaders with terrible Imposter Syndrome and the terrible imposters who should never have been allowed to lead.

As a senior director in Human Resources, Carolyn has pretty much seen it all, which is why she's often heard to say, *"Common sense isn't all that common"*.

Read this book to find out why!

Would you like to work with Carolyn Hobdey?

So, you've read the book . . . what next?

Being **yourSELF** won't happen overnight. It's not like flicking a switch. Changing your mindset and behaviours to step into being unapologetically you requires new habits; it takes many small actions, done consistently.

You're not alone. I'm here to walk with you as you continue your journey to Being yourSELF.

Visit www.carolynhobdey.com.

Here are some of your next steps options:

Want to dip your toe in the water of **SELFishness**?
Then start with *Redefining S.E.L.F.I.S.H.*, Carolyn's 7-part model that introduces practical ways to prioritise yourself through simple, easy-to-achieve activities.

Single S.E.L.F.I.S.H. element
Carolyn creates a safe space to guide you through a single element and get you started on your S.E.L.F.I.S.H. journey.

All S.E.L.F.I.S.H. elements
Looking for a short-cut to *Redefining S.E.L.F.I.S.H.*?
If you want optimal results in your busy life, then this deluxe option is perfect for you. Work through the entire S.E.L.F.I.S.H. model at your pace. Gain additional insights

and bespoke coaching designed especially for you and your life.

Ready to take *Being* **yourSELF** to the next level?
If you want to take control of your life by *Being Unapologetically yourSELF*, Carolyn will walk with you on the next phase of your story.

Single S.E.L.F. stage
Carolyn guides you through the Steps of the S.E.L.F. stage of your choice using discussion, mentoring and practical activities.

All S.E.L.F. stages
Keen to embrace a new you?
If you want maximum impact without going it alone, then this premium option is for you.

Work through all 12 S.E.L.F. Steps accessing additional activities and gaining deeper insights. Under Carolyn's guidance, this programme ensures you turn intentions into actions, so you get the unapologetic you—making you Mistress of your (mid)Life.

About the Author

Carolyn Hobdey is The Midlife Mistress: every woman's best friend at a time when she wants to take back control of her life.

She believes there is no need for your pleasure to be 'guilty'.

She is author of **All The Twats I Met Along The Way** and **Redefining SELFISH. No Guilt. No Regrets.** as well as co-author of **The Everyday Girls Guide to Living in Truth, Self-Love, and Acceptance**. Carolyn also has regular radio slots on WCRfm for 'Menopause Monday' and 'Humpday with Hobdey'.

Having lived a life of shame and blame, Carolyn now talks about 'Twats' in both senses of the word. On the one hand, tackling unhelpful mindsets and behaviours—and people—to enable you to be unapologetically you. On the other, being an advocate for women's health and wellbeing, with a particular specialism in the menopause.

As Founder of the transformational change business, MayDey Ltd, under which her professional portfolio sits, Carolyn is a regular speaker, trainer and media commentator on issues of toxic relationships and narcissism, self-esteem, identity and confidence, selfishness, women's health and menopause, and other imperative, topical women's issues.

With more than 20 years' experience as an award-winning Human Resources professional in some of the World's largest employers, Carolyn earned a seat at the boardroom table leading internationally recognised brands. Along the way—as well as meeting some Twats—a she gained a Masters in Lean Operations at Cardiff University, where she was the first HR specialist to undertake the course and became the winner of the inaugural Sir Julian Hodge Prize for Logistics, Operations and Manufacturing.

Carolyn has a lively life in Yorkshire, England and is a keen boxer, weightlifter, Latin and Ballroom dancer, car enthusiast, and singer.

WILHELM HANSEN EDITION
NR. 2841

Fantasistykker

Phantasiestücke

für Klavier und Klarinette (Violine)

Fantasias

for Piano and Clarinet (Violin)

af

Niels W. Gade

Op. 43

Edition Wilhelm Hansen, Copenhagen

Andantino con moto.

Niels. W. Gade, Op. 43.

Pianoforte.

Forlæggerens Eiendom.
ISBN 87 7455 130 2

Kjöbenhavn, Wilhelm Hansen.

4

537

6

8

BALLADE.

Tempo I.

riten. *tranquillamente.*

cresc. *mf* *f* *fz*

Ped. ✻

Ped. ✻

3537

14

Allegro molto vivace.

16

3537

SELECTED CHAMBER MUSIC

NIELS VIGGO BENTZON

Mosaique Musicale, op. 54, for flute, violin, cello and piano. Miniature score, parts.
String Quartet No. 3, op. 72. Miniature score, parts.
String Quartet No. 6, op. 124. Miniature score, parts.
Trio, op. 82, for trumpet, horn and trombone. Miniature score, parts.

LENNOX BERKELEY

Sextet, for clarinet, horn, and string quartet. Miniature score, parts.
String Quartet No. 2. Miniature score, parts.
Trio for violin, viola and cello. Miniature score, parts.

VAGN HOLMBOE

Quartetto Medico, op. 70, for flute, oboe, clarinet and piano. Miniature score, parts.
Quintet, op. 79, for 2 trumpets, horn, trombone and tuba. Miniature score, parts.

JØRGEN JERSILD

»Music-Making in the Forest«. Serenade for flute, oboe, clarinet, horn, bassoon. Miniature score, parts.

ERNST KRENEK

Trio, for violin, viola and cello. Miniature score, parts.

FRANCESCO G. MALIPIERO

Epodi e Gambi for violin, oboe, viola, violoncello. Miniature score, parts.
Quarto Quartetto, for string quartet. Miniature score, parts.

FINN MORTENSEN

Wind Quintet, for flute, oboe, clarinet, horn and bassoon. Miniature score, parts.
Trio, for violin, viola, cello. Miniature score, parts.

THEA MUSGRAVE

Serenade, for flute, clarinet, harp, viola, cello. Miniature score, parts.
String quartet. Miniature score, parts.

CARL NIELSEN

Wind Quintet, op. 43. Miniature score, parts.

PER NØRGÅRD

Fragment V, for violin and piano.
Quartetto Brioso, op. 21, for string quartet. Miniature score, parts.

FRANCIS POULENC

Sextet for piano, flute, oboe, clarinet, horn and bassoon. Miniature score, parts.
Sonata for horn, trumpet and trombone. Miniature score, parts.
Trio for piano, oboe and bassoon. Parts.

MATYAS SEIBER

Serenade for 2 clarinets, 2 bassoons, 2 horns. Miniature score, parts.

IGOR STRAVINSKY

Berceuses du Chat, for voice and 3 clarinets. Miniature score, parts.
Concertino for string quartet. Miniature score, parts.

EDITION WILHELM HANSEN